Young Hope

Playin' For Keeps

Young Hope

Young Hope

Copyright © 2012 Young Hope

All rights reserved.

ISBN: 0692398996
ISBN-13: 978-0692398999

Young Hope

DEDICATION

This book is dedicated to my beautiful mother Antoinette. Without her none of my successes would have been possible. And to my RNC team who've stood behind me this entire team and believed in me every step of the way. Shout out to all my Real Niggas, yall know who yall are. #RealNiggasNCorporated Or Nothin!!

Young Hope

RNC
Real Niggas N-Corporated

Young Hope

Young Hope

CHAPTER 1

Carlos was the average fifteen year old. He spent his time hanging with his crew and chasing young skirts without a care in the world. He was his mother, Priscilla's only child and they stayed in a modest two room apartment in San Diego, California. Everything was all peaches and cream until he got the fateful call informing him that Priscilla had died in a car wreck on her way home from work.

He went to go stay with his mother's parents in the small town of Hemet, California after the funeral, but that didn't last long. Carlo's grandparents were devout Christians and his wild ways quickly took its toll on them. It started out with a few school suspensions, but when the police brought him home one night after being caught with a couple of blunts, they had had enough.

The truth of the matter was, they were up in age and didn't really have the time to watch over a teenager. He didn't want to be there and they didn't want him there so they debated sending him to live with his father in St. Louis. Instead Los got in touch with his half-brother Victor and he sent for Los. He hopped on the Greyhound and two days later Victor was picking him up from the Greyhound station in St. Louis.

It was the beginning of summer so it was on and crackin'. Vic was twenty one and stayed in a four bedroom house on Wheaton Street right off of St. Charles Rock Road. He shared the house with three other nlggas. Latrell Scanes, bka Ever Since. They called him Ever since because he got in the dope game at nine years old and stayed down ever since.

Young Hope

Omar Olsen, bka O was a short fat black ass nigga with an annoying nasal voice. Los didn't know how, but the nigga kept bitches around. Terren Cole, bka T-KO was Vic's best friend. He was a five foot nine inch giant. It was rare to run into anybody who didn't know him. He had a wicked reputation in the streets for knocking niggas out and getting at shit with them guns. They were Vic's squad and that's what everybody called them. The Squad.

They cleared out the basement and set up a make shift room for Los. He wasn't tripping, he was just happy to be away from his grandparents and with some niggas more his speed. When Los got situated Vic pulled him up and took him shopping at Northwest Plaza in St. Ann. Los felt like he was walking with a celebrity or something because damn near everybody that worked at the mall knew him.

After Vic copped Los a couple fresh fits and pairs of shoes they went to the food court and ate while they caught up with each other. The last time they had seen each other was when Los was five before his mother took him out to Cali.

"You know I'm sorry to hear about your moms my nigga." Vic said in between bites of pizza.

"Yea. Me too." Los replied softly.

"I'm glad that you decided to come out here though. I want you to understand something if you don't already know this. Don't nobody give a fuck about your mama dyin'. The people of the world aint gone take nothing up off of you, so don't be expectin' sympathy from nobody. You damn sho aint get it from the squad. I aint tryna sound harsh and shit, I'm just telling you how it is cuz you my lil bro. Its time to man up and handle your wax."

"Don't nobody have to give a fuck. I give a fuck and that's all that matters."

"That's what I like to hear. But check this out. Livin' with me aint gone be a walk in the park. We got rules in the house. Follow the rules and you gone have fun. Disobey the rules and you more than likely gone end up getting your ass beat. Number one, no bitches live in our house. They more than welcome to spend the night or weekend, but there's a two day limit and they're gone. Number two, don't fuck wit nobody else's shit. Don't go in nobody's room and take nothing without asking and don't eat nobody else's food. Number three, clean up after yourself. And four, I'ma give you a minute to get adjusted, but you gone have to find some type of income. Everybody in the house pull they own weight.

"Aight. Best believe I'ma pull my own weight too."

"I know." From there it was on and crackin'. That night The Squad threw a party and Los had never seen so many bad bitches in one place. Vic introduced him to two chicken heads that were so bad Los' dick got hard just looking at them. "Ladies, this is my Lil bro, Los. He just got here this morning from Cali so I want ya'll to show him a good time, aight."

"Oh, I think we can deflnltelv do that." One of them said with a smile as Vic slid
Los a couple condoms. "Have fun my nigga."
"Good lookin' out." Los said before heading to the basement with the two dime pieces. That night he had his first threesome, but it definitely wouldn't be the last. The

next morning Vic woke Los up with a fat blunt.

"Get up. Pops wanna see you."

"Its on." About ten minutes later they were walking up the street smoking and
talking about the night before. When they got to a house with a black Range Rover in the drive way, Vic knocked on the door twice before a big ass nigga with two holsters on answered. He let them in and when they entered the living room Los was met by the biggest handgun he had ever seen in his life. His dad was aiming it right at Los' face with a black n mild hanging from his lips.

"Fuck you doin' in my house boy?" He asked in a gruff voice. Los put his hands up and looked back at Vic with a confused look on his face. "I'm just fuckin' wit you. How you doin' boy? You done got big." He said lowering the gun and hugging him. "I'm sorry to hear about ya mammy boy. She was a good woman. How ya brotha treatin' you?"

"Ok. I guess."

"Shit, better than ok. I got that Lil nigga two pieces of pussy last night." Vic said proudly.

"I likes that. I likes that. Look boy, if you need anything, I stay right here. A
closed mouth don't get fed, so don't be scared to ask."

"Aight. I appreciate that."

"I'd like to catch up with you, but Imma busy muhfucka, ya understand? We gone sit down when I get some time, but let me holla at ya broha real quick."

"Aight." Los turned to his bro. "I'll see you back at the house my nigga." He said before leaving. Just from the two minutes he was in his father's presence he could see why his mother left him. The nigga was a fuckin' weirdo, but from one look at the nigga Los could tell he was papered up. When Vic got back, Los was sitting on the couch chopping it up with Ever Since. Vic plopped down on the couch in between them and looked at Los.

"Say bro, that nigga fucked up. You can't really pay him no attention. Hell, the only reason I fuck wit that nigga is cuz he keep us all paid." Los shrugged it off.

"I aint trippin' my nigga. I don't even know that dude like that."

"And that's how you gotta treat that situation. But from me to you, that nigga is a trick and if you hit him up he gone break it off. Real shit." That summer set the standard for the rest of Los' life. Everybody in the house sold dope, but Los dragged his feet on getting in the game until one day when the motivation came from an unlikely source.

He was walking back from the liquor store on the corner when he saw an older chick named Jasmine sitting on her porch. She stayed right next door to them with her sister and her sister's baby daddy. Jasmine was a certified ten. She was bad, she hustled and she handled her business. Light skinned, petite, light brown eyes, hair and nails stayed tip top and she had a phat little apple bottom. Los walked up on her puffing on his black and mild like he was the shit. He stood over her and looked her right in the eyes.

"What up wit it Jazz? When you gone let a nigga put it in your life?" "Excuse me?" She asked with an uninterested smirk.

"When you gone let me put it in your life?"

"Boy, I'd eat your little ass alive. There's some little girls around the corner that's more your speed. You're a little cutie though, so I'll tell you what. When you start runnin' shit like your brother does, I'll put it in your life."

"Yea, you sho right."

"I know. You smoke?"

"Yea. Why, whats up?" She stood up and motioned for him to come inside with her.

"Make yourself comfortable. I'll be right back." Los sat down on the couch as she headed towards the back of the house. About two minutes later she re-emerged with a fat blunt and a couple little baggies in her hand. She dropped the bags in Los' lap. "That's a fifty sack of purp and some seeds. Go grow a couple plants or something." She said as she lit the blunt.

"Good lookin'."

"Fa sho. What are you, in middle school?"

"Naw, I'm bout to be a sophomore." He replied as she handed him the blunt. "Huh. I'm telling you, you stay on deck with that shit, all kinds of Lil bitches gone be throwin' the pussy at you."

"Well, what I gotta do to fuck wit you?"

"Grow up baby boy." When Los left Jasmine's house he went straight to his backyard and planted a couple seeds back behind the house out of the reach of Vic's two blue nosed pits. He got on the internet an found out how to grow the plants correctly and by the time school started, he was on deck with his first batch. Vic enrolled Los in University City High and Los loved every minute of it. He had never been to a predominately black school before, so he was really digging that shit.

On his first day he was sitting in computer class when he over heard a few girls asking a nigga where they could buy some week from. He went in his back pack pulled out a fifty sack that was already bagged up, leaned in between the computers and chunked the sack on to one of the girls keyboards. She quickly snatched it up and looked at him.

"What's this?"

"Some purp." He stated matter of factly.

"What you want for it?" She asked as she held it underneath her nose. "That shit right there is fifty dollars a gram and that's a gram right there." "Fifty dollars for this?"

"That aint no reggie mama, that's purp. But check me out. I'll let you get if for twenty five bucks, just let ya friends know who got the finest." She sat there thinking about it with a goofy grin on her face. Her home girl spoke up.

"What's your name Boo Boo?" "Los, and you are?"

"I'm Denise and this is Nancy. I think Ima take you up on your offer." She said as she dug in her pocket. She pulled out a twenty and Nancy produced a five dollar bill. When they gave Los the money the nigga they had been talking to walked over and sat next to him.

Young Hope

"Let me get one of them."

"What you got?" Los asked as he stuck the money in his pocket. "Nothin'." Los started laughing.

"Well I aint got shit for you my nigga." "Lil nigga, I'll take yo shit!"

"On my dead mama rest in peace, you aint gone enjoy it nigga. All I can say is go for what the fuck you know." Los said looking the nigga straight in the eyes.

"T-Rock, leave that nigga alone. He aint do nothing to you." Denise said. T-Rock slowly stood up, the whole time grilling Los. It took everything in him not to knock a hole in the nigga's face. He wasn't about to get into a fight with all that weed in his back pack. Later on that day Los went into the restroom on the third floor to take a piss. He handled his business and as he finished washing his hands T'Rock and two other niggas walked in.

"Awe shit. This is the bitch ass nigga I was telling ya'll about." He said slapping one of his boys in the chest with the back of his hand.

"Let me see that back pack Lil nigga." The tallest of the three said. Los took off his back pack and threw it at the nigga's chest. When he went to catch it he caught a hard right hook. The tall nigga stumbled back, dazed and T-Rock got rocked with a wild left over hand followed by an uppercut. The bathroom was so small that the third nigga couldn't do anything but fall back up against the wall, behind his home boys.

Los went to work getting a t the two niggas like

his life depended on it. He couldn't hold the momentum though. The third nigga broke free and caught Los with some wild shit that pushed him back. The tall nigga was still dazed, but T•Rock recovered and the fight quickly turned ugly for Los. He held his own, but he was no match for both of them together.

The door swung open behind them and a big nigga with braids walked into the bathroom. He watched Los lock with the two niggas for a few seconds and then out of the blue he hit T-Rock in the back of the head so hard that the nigga dropped like a fly. He then stumbled the tall nigga with a left hook giving Los enough room to serve him with a vicious two piece that sent him to the ground. When he tried to get up, Los grabbed the back of his head and rammed his knee into his face knocking him out cold.

The big nigga turned around and the other nigga put his hands up in surrender. The big nigga served him with a straight right that slumped him in the corner. Somebody else walked into the restroom and stopped dead in his tracks. He looked at the three niggas laid out, then at Los and the big nigga and turned around and left out. Los snatched up his back pack and motioned for his new found patna to follow him. They left out of the restroom just as the bell rung. Los turned to the nigga and shook his hand.

"Yo good lookin' out my nigga."

"Don't lean on it. You was handlin' ya business in there though. I likes that plus I don't fuck with that bitch ass nigga T-Rock anyway. I been wantin' a reason to serve that clown."

"Well I'm glad you showed up when you did. What's

ya name my nigga?"

"They call me Ace."

"I'm Los."

"Aye. Get to your classes. The bell rung already." A black security guard said as he came up the stairs.

"We on it man." Ace said. He looked at Los." Where you headed?" "Mrs. Shapiro. Honors English." Ace frowned up and smiled.

"Me too." During class they chopped it up and the two instantly clicked. It was the beginning of a strong friendship that would last for years. Los chunked him half a zip of purp for looking out and made plans to fuck with him outside of school. He texted Vic and told him what happened, so the squad was there in front of the school waiting after school. As soon as Los walked over Vic and T-Ko bombarded him with questions.

"Where them bitch ass niggas at?" T-Ko asked scanning the crowd of people streaming out of the school. When T-Rock came out he froze in place and Los pointed him out.

"There he go right there."

"Thomas?" Vic asked in surprise. "Get the fuck outta here. Come on bro." Vic, T-Ko, Ever Since, O and Los walked up on T-Rock in front of the school. Everybody around started watching. "You fuckin' wit my lil bro nigga?" Vic asked getting in his face.

"It look like he the one that got jumped." O joked

pointing out the visible lumps on T-Rock's forehead and his swollen lips.

"Look lil nigga. Don't fuck wit my bro. you betta ask yo big bro and counsin's how I get down. This really aint what ya'll want. On my mama."

"Let's roll my nigga. These Lil niggas aint on nothing. Lil bro done already put em in they place." T-Ko said putting his hand on Vic's shoulder. "But aye, Thomas or whatever your name is, don't make us come back up here man. I'd hate to have yellow police tape all around this bitch, ya dig." Everybody watched as they all hopped in a black Expedition and dipped out. First impressions were everything and Los left his mark out the gate.

Chapter 2

That Saturday Los caught the bus out to U-City to fuck with Ace. He stayed right up the street from the school, so his house wasn't that hard to find. He was really out of pocket, so he hit Vic up and got a 16 shot 45 from him. He liked to fight, but he wasn't going to get jumped again. When he got to Ace's house he rang the doorbell and was surprised when Denise answered.

"Denise? You live here?"

"Yea. What are you doing here?"

"I thought that nigga Ace lived here. I was tryna fuck with him." "He does. That's my brother. Come in."

"I ain't know that shit." Los said as he walked into the living room. "So what ya'll got going on?" Los shrugged his shoulders.

"Nothin' really. Why, what's up?" She shook her head. "I was just asking."

"You tryna get on a blunt with me and you bro?"

"Sure, why not. Let me go get him real quick." She turned around and made a show of switching extra hard as she headed down the hallway. She was cute and had a fat lil ass, but being around his bro broke him of fucking with girls his age. They just didn't interest him like a full grown woman did. But he would fuck her if the opportunity came up.

"What up boy." Ace greeted as he entered the living room with Denise close behind him.

"What up with it. Ya'll be smoking in the house?"

Young Hope

"Man, fuck naw. My moms in the back sleep. We gone have to go hit a couple blocks."

"Aight. I told ya sister she could roll." Ace shrugged his shoulders.

"Whatever. Come on." When they got outside Los pulled a blunt out of his black in mild box and lit it up.

"You know you's a bold ass nigga Los. You just rode the bus out here by yourself like eve hing everything. You know them niggas really want your head." Los laughed and raised up his shirt flashing his burner.

"What type of nigga you take me for man? Them niggas come fuckin' wit me Ima do em off the flop, not extras." He said as he handed the blunt to Ace. Denise just walked along in silence eyeing Los. He peeped her out, but he didn't pay her any attention.

"What's that a 45?"

"Yea."

"I got a chrome snub nosed .357 back at the house. No shells, no evidence my nigga." Ace bragged.

"That's right."

"You tryna push over the homie Jay house?" "He straight?"

"He is to me, but I can't put my opinion off on you my nigga."

"Fuck it. Let's go. I trust your judgment." When they got to Jay's house he was sitting on the porch with another nigga listening to music. They walked up and Ace introduced Los to the two niggas.

"What up with it Jay. Aye, remember that nigga I was telling you about? The one from the bathroom. This dude, Los this my guy Jay."

"What up." Los said as he shook the nigga's hand.

"And this piece of shit over here is Moe." Jay had a real laid back demeanor. And he looked like Sean Paul from the Young Bloodz. Moe was an ugly ass nigga with two gold teeth and kinky ass afro.

"My nigga told me that you was seein' shit." Jay said.

"It wasn't shit."

"Hell yea. You be deckin' with that purp too, huh?"

"I do what I can. Why, what's up?"

"If it the real deal then, you just got yourself a loyal customer." He said sittin forward in his chair.

"Oh it is. We just put one in the air on the way over here." Denise added. Los pulled out his last blunt, which he was saving for later on and tossed it to Jay.

"Why don't you tell me if it's the real deal or not." They vibed off the flop and pretty soon Los found himself fucking around in U-City more than he was at home. He was getting his money up off the purp and one day he was in the car with Ace, Moe and Jay when he saw a black old school Caprice parked on the street with a for sale sign in the window.

"Aye stop." He said hitting the back of the driver seat.

"What up man?" Moe asked as he hit the brakes. Los hopped out the car and ran up to the house and rung the doorbell. A few seconds later a fat nigga answered the door with a beer in his hand.

"What up with it? You don't know me, but I just saw that for sale sign on that Caprice. What you tryna sell it for?"

"Twenny five hunnet." He stated plainly. "You interested?"

"Yea. I'll be back tomorrow to get it." He said before turning around and leaving. Los had Moe take him to his dad's house. "Ya'll just post up. I'll be right back."

"Man hurry up." Moe said obviously agitated.

"Nigga you act like you got something to do or something." Los said as he got out the car. He went up to the house, knocked a couple times then just walked in. He heard some voices coming from the kitchen so he went in there and saw his father posted with his bodyguard, a bitch and some other loud mouth nigga. Alabaster saw his son standing there and started smiling.

"How you get in here?"

"The door was unlocked." Alabaster slapped his bodyguard in the back of the head.

"Go fuckin' fix that shit." He barked and the big nigga quickly left the kitchen. Alabaster looked back at

Los. "What you want boy?"

"Let me holla at you in private man."

"You can holla right here." Los looked at the bitch and the loud mouth nigga then back at his dad.

"Aight. You said if I needed anything, ask. Well I need twenty five hundred dollars."

"For what?" He asked as he grabbed a beer out of the refrigerator. "A car."

"Ya'll young niggas don't work for shit nowadays. Ya'll always want a got damn hand out. When I was comin' up we had to work for everything we wanted." The loud mouth nigga interjected. Los shot him a sideways glance before replying.

"You need to mind your own fuckin' bitness. Didn't nobody ask you for your fuckin' opinion nigga." He turned back to Alabaster. "Who is this nigga?"

"Chuck. A golden gloves boxer and twenty five hundred says you can't fuck with him." Alabaster replied with a grin as he sipped his beer. Los looked at Chuck then hauled off and served him right in his shit. Chuck fell back up against the counter when two more hard fists connected with his face. He tried to grab Los, but he knocked his arms away and hit him with an uppercut that buckled his knees. When Chuck fell, Los kicked him in his stomach then pulled out his pistol, dropped to his knees and commenced to pistol whipping Chuck's face.

"Aye boy! What the fuck you doin'?" Alabaster

asked, half laughing. "Come on with that shit there. You getting blood all over my got damn floor!" Los wiped the blood off of his gun onto Chuck's shirt, then stood up.

"You was actin' like you wanted a show, so I gave you a fuckin' show."

"Don't take that tone with me boy. I'll wear your lil ass out." Alabaster said pointing at Los with his bottle.

"Sounds good. Where my money at?" Alabaster busted up laughing and looked at the bitch who just stood there dead silent.

"Do me a favor and clean this shit up." He said before putting his hand on Los' shoulder. "Come on Lil nigga." He led Los into the basement and flicked on the lights. He walked over to a big ass green safe in the far corner. "Who taught you how to fight like that boy?" He asked as he put in the combination.

"Nobody. It just comes naturally."

"Yea. You just like I was when I was yo age." Los stared at Alabaster like yea right as he opened up the safe. Alabaster pulled out a stack and tossed it to Los. "That's five grand right there, so you aint gotta come fuckin' with me no mo. You need to come get you a sack while you bullshittin'."

"I'm doin' my own thing right now." Alabaster slammed the safe shut.

"I heard, but there aint no real money in that shit. When you ready to step ya game up I'll be right here."

"Let me get back to you on that. But look my ride outside, preciate the funds." Alabaster waved Los off dismissively. The next day Los was pushing his first whip. The first thing he did was throw a sound system in it, and he was feeling like the shit. His dad's words always echoed in his head though, so one day when he was sitting in the spot with Jay and Ace he asked them how much they paid for a zip.

"Shit, seven fifty if a nigga can get some love, but a nigga usually pay about eight. Why? You tryna get on?"

"Naw, I was just askin'." When he got home he pushed up on Ever Since with the same question.

"Nigga, I aint bought a zone in so long, but fuckin' with your pops we be getting em for five. Why? You Lil bad ass tryna get on?"

"Yea. I got a g right now. What's up?"

"Man, let me holla at Vic. He aint finna be at my throat about this shit." They called Vic and he laughed at Los.

"What you tryna do lil bro?"

"I'm tryna stack. Ya'll fuckin' wit me or what?"

"Hold up. Put Ever Since back on real quick." They talked for a few minutes and when Ever Since got off the phone he took Los in the kitchen and gave him a crash course on the dope game. Most of it he already knew, but Ever Since gave him a few pointers on how to cook it up in the microwave and bring back them extras. When they were done they turned the two ounces of soft into seventy one grams of crack.

"You finna shoot to the spot?" Ever Since asked as Los sat at the table and cut up an ounce.

"The homies over there in U-City got a cool Lil spot. Ima go post up over there."

"Aight nigga. Be safe and remember you aint from over there. Them niggas might seem cool and I aint sayin' they aint, but when you start ballin' around them niggas they gone start actin' funny with you. That's just how niggas is." Los nodded his head in agreement.

"They won't be actin' funny if they ballin' too." He said with a smile.

"Probably not, but remember what I said."
"I will my nigga." Rockets don't even take off as fast as Los did. Out of that extra half a zip he cooked up he gave Jay and Ace a quack a piece just on GP. The next week he was literally playing with a four and a half burning dope in the microwave trying to learn the best way to cook the shit. The young nigga had as much money he didn't know what to do with it all.

He flipped the Caprice. Threw some 23 inch rims on, had it beating out of control with a few screens in it and hit the mall up almost daily. Vic had to pull him up.

"Look lil nigga. You doin' ya thang and that's cool, but you ridin' around in that hot ass Chevy dirty than a muthafucka and you aint even attempted to get your L's or insure that bitch. You just gone have to be salty, but you aint drivin' that shit no more til you get your shit together. Give me your keys."

"This is some bullshit."

"I don't wanna be the bad guy, but if you get pulled over and knocked, it'll be my fault."

"I won't."

"Give me your fuckin' keys nigga." Vic demanded and Los reluctantly handed over his keys. It was hard going back to taking the bus so Los hurried up and got legal. He understood why Vic did what he did, but he was still salty at him, so he avoided being around him as much as possible. One night Los had been in the spot all night and had dozed off until Denise walked in and woke him up.

"Los, Los wake up." She said with a sense of urgency in her voice as she nudged him in the chest. Los slowly sat up rubbing his face.

"What up lil mama?"

"Look!" Los looked down and frowned up as his mind processed the situation. Both of his pockets had been cut open and emptied. He quickly stood up patting himself down. His pistol was still on his hip, but his money, dope and cell phone were gone.

"What the fuck?" He looked around. "Where the fuck is Moe?" "I don't know. I just walked in."

"Maaaaan." He walked to the bathroom and there Moe was getting his dick sucked by a smoker. "Moe, what the fuck man!"

"What?" He asked incredulously.

"I got fuckin' robbed. That's what. I fuckin' dozed off and you just fuckin' left a nigga out there! Dumb ass nigga!"

"What was I supposed to do?" Moe asked with his arms out as the smoker got up off her knees.

"You shoulda woke him up." Denise chimed in from the doorway. Los let out a deep sigh before turning and leaving with Denise hot on his heels. He went outside and just started walking up the street. "Where are you going?"

"I don't fuckin' know." They walked past two niggas who were standing on the corner when Los heard his ring tone. He looked over at the niggas and sure enough one of them had his phone in their hand. "Aye patna, where the fuck you get that phone from?"

"None of you got damn busi......... " Los drew down on him and snatched the phone from him." That old smoker Robert. He just sold it to a nigga like two minutes ago." He said with his hands up.

"Where he at?"

"He went to the park to smoke man." Los took off running towards the hood park. When he got there Robert was sitting on the swings sucking on a glass dick. He didn't even see Los coming, he just felt a sharp pain in the back of his head as Los racked him with his burner.

"Bitch ass nigga! You gone try to rob me?" Los yelled as Robert fell to the ground and tried to scramble away.

"Naw.... naw man I was just testin' you."

"What?!" Los lost it. He started stomping and kicking Robert as hard as he could.

"Los wait!!" Denise screamed as she finally bent the corner with the two niggas who had Los cell phone.

"Testin' me? Bitch nigga I'll kill you!" He said through gritted teeth as he stomped Robert's face in. Denise ran up and grabbed him from behind.

"Stop. You're going to kill him." Los shook loose from Denise and emptied Robert's pockets, then stepped on his wrists and shot him in both hands.

"Test that! Pussy!" He spat before turning around and walking away. He learned that night that slippers counted and that mistake was never made again. But Ace was just as new to the game as Los was and he learned that same lesson in a different way. He was out with some chicken head shinning and flashing his knot and the wrong muthafuckas saw it. They were in the parking lot of a run down soul food joint when six niggas ran up on him with their thumps out.

"Aye bitch nigga, empty them pockets out. Try something slick and you aint gone make it home tonight." Ace looked them all in, memorizing each of their faces as he pulled all of the money from his pockets. He recognized one of the niggas. It was T-Rock.

"What the fuck you lookin' at bruh? Take that chain off!" T-Rock said as he pressed the barrel of his gun up against Ace's temple. "I oughta smoke you nigga, but Ima let you live." He hit Ace over the head and the rest of his crew rushed him. He took the ass whooping in stride, because he knew if he fought back he'd get shot to shit.

Later that night when he got home Denise saw his face and wigg_ed out. The first thing she did was call Los and twenty minutes later Los, Moe and Jay were at their house strapped and ready for action.
"What the fuck happened?" Jay asked as everybody looked at Ace's swollen face. "That nigga T-Rock and them robbed and jumped me." He said before putting his head down. Jay, Los and Moe all looked at each other.

"Well, what the fuck you sittin' there for? Get yo big ass up and come on." Los said getting hot.

"What you mean, for what? We finna go find them niggas and take it to em." "Straight up." Moe added. Ten minutes later they were in a smoker's bucket in traffic. First they went by the soul food joint, then they rode around that muthafucka for about twenty minutes before riding out by where T-Rock's mother stayed.

"If we don't find this nigga tonight, we shootin' up his mama shit." Los said as he stared out the front passenger side window. As soon as those words left his mouth he spotted T-Rock and four other niggas walking up the street. It was dark as hell outside, but Los saw Ace's chain hanging around 'I-Rock's neck and the way he walked was a dead giveaway. "There they bitch asses go right there!" He exclaimed as he rolled down his window.

They wee so busy laughing and joking each other that they didn't even see the car pulling up on them, Los, Jay and Ace all hung out he windows with pistols in hand.

"I told you, you wouldn't enjoy the shit nigga!" Los

yelled before they all opened fire. Each one of the four niggas walking with T-Rock got hit, but God must have been with him that night because he walked away unscathed. That shit started a deadly feud that wouldn't come to a head until years later.

Chapter 3

By the time Los graduated from high school and turned eighteen he was dealing with half a brick. He could have had a couple birds easy, but he was content with what he was pushing. He had his niggas on deck serving them for cheap so they all bubbled like soap suds. It was a beautiful thing and the four of them had solidified their position in the streets.

Los was getting his grown man on, but on the inside he was still a Lil nigga. He had enough cake to buy his own crib, but he stayed in the basement, Vic didn't mind, but he didn't understand it either. When he was coming up in the game he hurried up and got out of the house with Alabaster. It just wasn't shit like having your own and Los had a lot of shit just not a crib.

One day he was at the mall splurging on unnecessary shit with his crew. He had just made a mold for his grill at a jewelry booth when a group of girls walked past them. One girl in particular stood out. They made eye contact and Lost couldn't turn away. She was short, light skinned, thick and classy. The way she strutted past them had Los captivated. Without even thinking he reached out and gently grabbed her hand.

"Excuse me mama. I don't mean no disrespect, grabbin' you and shit, but you beautiful than a muthafucka and if I aint say something I'd regret it later on down the line."

"Thank you." She said as she started blushing.

"You're more than welcome. What's your name?" He asked still holding her hand. His crew and her home girls all just stood around watching them, hanging on to every word.

"Amaya. And you are?"

"Carlos, but everybody calls me Los. Now I'm prayin' that you don't, but I just know that some lucky ass nigga is claimin' you "

"Actually, I haven't found anybody that lucky yet."

"So then it would be aight if I got your number.... "

"I think that would be aight." She replied with a smile. "You got a pen." Los handed her his phone and she punched her number in and saved it before giving it back.

"Ima be expectin' a call."

"And Ima most definitely be callin' you." They hugged and when the girls walked off Los playfully hit Ace in the chest. "Ya'll niggas whack. Why ya'll aint get at them other hoes?"

"Hell, I was takin' notes." Moe joked.

"Well, what can I say man. Ima player by nature. Ima take her, lace her and have her beatin' her feet like a waiter, ya dig?" He popped like he was on some pimp shit.

"Get the fuck outta here nigga. You don't know the first thing about pimpin'." Jay said looking at Los.

"Pst, watch." A few days later Los called Amaya and hooked up with her. He took her out to dinner at Sweetie Pies, then they just rolled around in his Caprice and chopped it up. They smoked a couple blunts and she opened up to him. She told him how her mother died from a heroine overdose when she was five and how she ended up in foster care after her father raped her and she ran away.

She was only nineteen, but she had been through some shit. All of her relationships were the same, because she was eye candy her boyfriends always seemed to be insecure and that would result in here getting her ass beat. She knew where she wanted to go in life, she just didn't know how she was going to get there. Because of her trust issue she lived alone and she had a wack ass job at Albertson's, so she basically lived check to check.

It was sad, but it didn't inspire any sympathy. Even though Amaya was an interesting girl all Los saw was a piece of pussy. But she had that shit locked down. Los made it clear that he wasn't trying to be her nigga, so she kept her legs closed. That didn't deter Los, it just made him want to knock her even more. He went extra hard in her ear until all she could think about was being with him, then he backed up off of her.

When she called he'd act like he was busy or he'd let another bitch answer the phone. That shit drove her crazy until one night she texted him, telling him to come over. When Los got there Amaya answered the door wearing a black Victoria Secret set with Usher's "Nice and Slow" playing on the stereo in the living room. He picked her up as he started kissing her and kicked the door closed.

Los carried her into the living room and laid her down on the couch. The look of anticipation in her eyes had his manhood standing at attention. He dropped his burner on the carpet as he took off his shirt. When he undressed Amaya he stood there for a few seconds admiring her beautiful body. He wasn't too fond of eating pussy, but he was going to turn her all the way out. Los licked her up and down and by the time he strapped on the magnum, she was soaking wet.

Los moved her to the floor and went in deep like he was digging for gold. She gasped for air as he grabbed hold of her ass and began to hit her with long deliberate strokes. He started off slow then started beating it up like a real nigga was supposed to. Ten minutes later Amaya was screaming at the top of her lungs as an orgasm rocked her body.

"Oh my God! Carlos, stay right there." She moaned as she began to meet him thrust for thrust until she came again. Los pulled out, picked her up and bent her over the couch. He slapped her on the ass then ran up in her from behind trying his best to knock down her walls. "Uhh your killin' me!!" She screamed as Los plowed into her repeatedly. Amaya tried to run from him, but he held onto her thighs and continued to hawk her down.

Amaya had never felt pain like the pain Los was inflicting on her, but she liked it. She started throwing it back at him and he grabbed a handful of her hair and yanked her head back. Los was giving it to her raw and uncut and when he felt himself about and to cum he pulled out, pulled the condom off, turned Amaya around and busted all over her face.

From then on Amaya was like Los' shadow. She was head over heels in love with the nigga and would do anything for him. When they were in traffic together she would have his dope sack stuffed and when he had shit to do she'd sit off in the spot and serve for him. The shit was funny to Ace and Jay, but Moe was light weight hatin' on him. Los didn't give a fuck. He was doing him and in a superb way.

Amaya was on deck, but Los wanted to see if he could actually get her to sell some pussy for him. He knew a lot of nigga's and they were always on him about how bad she was and what they'd do to her. But if Los had anything to do with it the only thing they would be doing is paying her, which in turn would be getting him paid. One night after Los put the pipe down on her they sat up in bed chopping it up.

"So you aint never had a real girlfriend?" She asked with her head on his chest.

"Naw. I just can't myself with a girl that don't know how significant she is." "What you mean?"

"Like I know what I want and I know how to get it, but most of the bitches I run across always want this and that, but they dependin' on a nigga to get it for them. They don't even know what they pussy worth."

"And what's is my pussy worth?" She asked sitting up to look at him.

"Your pussy is priceless." He said before kissing her. "I could run outta dope, then where my money gone come from? But you can't run out of pussy. That shit aint goin' nowhere and everybody want it. It's millions of muthafuckas out there that's willin' to pay top dollar for what you got in between your legs. Niggas be askin' me about you everyday."

"I don't know why. I aint no hoe."

"Who called you a hoe? Look, let me break something down to you mama. Hoe's are trifling. They nasty and they fuck for free. Hoes be out there fuckin' just to be fuckin', so I personally would never refer to you as a hoe or let anybody else disrespect you like that. All I'm sayin' is there's a lot of niggas ready to break off their hard earned money just for you to straddle they laps. If a bitch wanted to pay me for ten, fifteen minutes of my time, I'd take advantage of that shit." He gamed. "Shit, you got some good pussy, so half them niggas wouldn't even last five minutes. That's highway robbery."

"If I was to do that, what would you be? My pimp?"

"Do I look like a pimp? I would be your business manager slash financial advisor." Amaya laid her head back down on Los' chest.

"I trust you baby. If you promise nothings' happen to me, I'll do it."

"Cross my heart and hope to die." A few days later Los hooked her up with her first John, a nigga named Marco from L-Wood. Los rented a room at the North West Inn and sat in the living room playing x-Box while Amaya handled her business in the room. Ten minutes later Marco emerged sweating profusely like he had just finished running a marathon. He nodded at Los and left as Amaya came out of the room with a childish grin on her face.

One day Los and Ace were sitting off in the spot clockin' when Amaya came through with a sexy Lil Mexican chick. She was about 5'5", with long brown hair, a petite frame and an ass like a black woman. She could have been a double for the singer Cassie.

"Hey daddy." Amaya beamed as they walked through the door.

"Got damn, who is this?" Ace asked as they both checked out the new girl. "This is Magdelena. I met her over there at the Scottish Inn in St. Ann." "Ok. Well, what she doin' here?"

"Her employer aint been doing her right and we been seeing each other around. I just told her that I'd introduce her to you." Los stood up and walked up on the new girl.

"So you tryna get down with the team?"

"Si, papi." She replied as she stood there nervously. Los walked around her scanning her body with his eyes.

"You can't be dressin' like that. That's some bullshit." He said gesturing towards her hot pink dress and stilettos. He looked at Amaya, "baby girl, take her and clean her up aight, and when you do, bring her over here." Los turned to Ace, "you tryna test drive this?"

"You got damn straight." He said blowing a kiss at Magdelena. "Aight. Go handle ya business and come back."

"Ok." Amaya said before kissing Los on the check and leaving with Magdelena close behind her.

"When did you start doin' it like that nigga?" Ace asked as Los sat back down on the couch. Los shrugged.

"I just tell them bitches pay me or pay me no attention, ya dig?" "Man shut the fuck up." They both busted up laughing.

Chapter 4

Ever since and Vic walked into the house from a long night in the streets and were met with a strong aroma coming from the kitchen. When they went into the kitchen Amaya and Magdelena were cooking breakfast wearing nothing but T-shirts.

"Ok. Who the fuck are ya'll?" Vic asked as he glanced at his watch to se that it was 7:15 am.

"Oh, I'm Amaya and this is Magdelena. Los said it would be alright if we cooked everybody breakfast. We're almost done." Ever Since and Vic both looked at each other dumbfounded. Magdelena went into the refrigerator and bent over giving them a straight shot. When she turned around she smiled, she asked, "are you guys hungry?"

"Yea what ya'll in here cookin'?" Ever Since asked as he walked up behind her. Vic shook his head and nodded at Amaya.

"Where Los at?"

"Downstairs." Vic headed for the door that led to the basement and descended the stairs. He instantly spotted Los sitting on his bed with money scattered all around him. He was counting it and dividing it into stacks of a thousand.

"Fuck you got goin' on lil nigga?" Vic asked as he walked up on Los, scanning the basement with his eyes. There was a stripper pole in the corner, a camera sitting on a tripod facing it and Amaya and Magdelena's clothes all over the floor. "What's up wit them bitches?"

"They bad aint they?" Los asked with a big kool-aid grin on his face. "They my employees bro."

"Employees? You pimpin'?" Vic asked incredulously.

"Naw, I'm just instructin' them. Pimpin' is dead my nigga."

"They sellin' pussy for you?"

"Yea, among other things ..... "

"Well, you pimpin' then Lil nigga. I can't fuckin' believe this shit." Vic started laughing. "My Lil nigga got some hoes."

"Employees my nigga." He corrected.

"Whatever. What you doin' over here with this camera and pole?" "Makin' a movie. That shit finna get a nigga paid."

"It look like your funds is already healthy." Vic said gesturing towards the bed.

"There's always room for improvement. But what's up with you and Ever Since? Ya'll niggas been MIA and shit."

"Oh yea. Shits bout to change my nigga. Pops like he leavin' the game alone." "And. I don't fuck with that nigga no way." Los said as he began to count out another stack.

"He leavin' me the plug so now Ima be the nigga holdin' the cards and I went and looked at this house in Belleville. I'm thinking bout letting' you get this muthafucka." Los looked up.

"You serious?"

"It aint official yet, but if everything go right its gone be on."

"What about O and them?"

"Everybody movin'. What you think niggas gone live together forever?" Sure enough a few weeks later everybody started to file out of the house one by one and Jay, Ace and Moe moved in to replace them. When Vic got on with the plug he threw Los a brick off the flop and he sat him down for a heart to heart.

"Aight lil nigga. It's a different ball game now. I aint gone be here to hold your hand, so it's time for you to man up...."

"I been...." Vic cut him off.

"Shut up and listen. Like I said it's time for you to man up. You been handlin' your business, but you been sheltered the whole time. Whether you know it or not me and my niggas been watchin' everything ya'll do. I can't be there like that no more cuz I aint gone be in the position to. Don't get it twisted nigga, I'll die for you, but with what I got gain' on now I gotta fall back off the hot shit and get this money.

"Now, this is your house. Them niggas livin' in them three rooms is your soldiers. You the leader of this squad and you gotta make sure they understand that shit. Fuck all that we equal shit. It don't work like that. You control the dope so you in charge just don't run around like your shit don't stank cuz ya'll niggas gone need to depend on each other, and if you get to tryna push your weight around they gone gang up on you. I done seen it too many times." Los just sat there soaking up the game.

"When Pops had the connect he was just doin' us any old type of way, but now that I got it, we gone get rich my nigga. That first one free, but from now on Ima need twenty racks a piece."

"Aight. Let's get it crackin' then." Los hit everybody off with a nine piece and told them to bring back five racks for the re-up money, then he split a four and a half between Amaya and Magdelena. They had started snorting the shit, but a lot of the tricks were spending top dollar to get high with them. The money literally flooded in and Los was really feeling himself.

He went and bought a black Lexus and had it rigged with a stash box. He stopped driving and had Amaya or Magdelena drive him around. He made everybody else buy black cars and when he started rocking black clothes all of his niggas followed suit. When they came through muthafuckas started calling them the Black Crew and the shit stuck.

A lot of niggas didn't like how Los and his crew did their thing. The main hater was T-Rock. He had his own little crew, but they weren't really factors in the street like that. They sold dope, but mostly all they did was try to rob muthafuckas and that made niggas not want to do business with them. Even though T-Rock hated on Los' crew they really didn't come into contact to much until one day when Los got a surprise visit from a stranger.

They were all at the house fucking around when somebody started pounding on the door like a psycho. Ace and Moe snatched their guns of the coffee table and went to see who it was. When Ace looked out the peephole he saw a sexy caramel toned bitch standing on the porch with another uglier bitch behind her. Ace tucked his pistol into his jeans and opened the door.

"What up baby?"

"Don't baby me nigga." She snapped. "Los stay here?"

"Aye bitch, you can kick rock with all that attitude and shit."

"Bitch? I got yo bitch nigga! Tell Los punk ass to come out here." Ace tried to slam the door in her face, but she put her foot in the way. "Uh-uh. Where that nigga at?!"

"Get the fuck from over here before a nigga have to fuck yo Lil ass up!" Ace growled as he approached her.

"Nigga touch me and ima have my brother kill yo trick ass."

"Fuck you and your brother, bitch!" Ace pushed her making her stumble back into the other bitch.

"Hold up my nigga. What's going on?" Los asked as he grabbed Ace's arm and walked onto the porch. When the aggressive bitch regained her balance she stared Los down like he was dipped in shit.

"You Los?"

"Yea why?" She tried to swing off on him, but he side stepped the punch with his hands up. Ace stepped up, but Los shook his head telling him no.

"What the fuck is wrong with you girl?"

"What's wrong with me is you got my fuckin' home girl Amaya fuckin' hoe'n for you nigga!" That's when he recognized her. She was with Amaya in the mall when he had first met her.

"That aint none of your fuckin' business lil mama."

"To hell it aint. You gone leave her the fuck alone or Ima have my brother get at yo muthafuckin' ass."

"Again with the brother shit. Who is this nigga?" Ace asked.

"T-Rock!" She stated matter of factly. Los, Ace and Moe looked at each other then busted up laughing, as Amaya walked out onto the porch to see what was going on. "Amaya! What are you doin' with this nigga?"

"Like I said that aint none of your business."

"Cynthia, what are you doing here?" Amaya asked.

"I came to get you."

"She aint goin' no where. Now move around before I remove you." Los said as calmly as he could.

"Fuck you bitch!" She spat and as soon as the words rolled off her tongue Los back handed the shit out of her.

"Now go get yo bitch ass brother and you gone fuckin' get him killed on my mama. Get the fuck off my porch!" Cynthia held her bleeding lip as she turned around and ran for her car with the other bitch close behind her.

"Los you didn't have to hit her." Amaya said as she watched her ex-home girl drive off. Los lifted his hand to her like he was about to send her one.

"Bitch, you the reason she was even over here. Now Ima have to lay this ol buster ass nigga down behind this shit. Get the fuck out my face before I break yours."

****

T-Rock was sitting at the kitchen table at his mama's house when Cynthia stormed in with tears in her eyes and a fat busted lip. He stood up frowning as she started sobbing.

"What the hell? Who did this?"

"That bitch ass nigga Los slapped me." "What?! Where you run into that nigga at?"

"I went to his house".

"Fuck was you doin' at his house?" He asked as he snatched up his pistol and cocked it back.

"I went to get my home girl and he slapped me." T-Rock brushed past her and left the house. He called up a couple of his niggas and they headed over to Jay's spot. Los had called him and told him what was up so he was walking to his car when T-Rock and his boys bent the corner in a smoker bucket. Jay pulled out his sixteen shot Berretta and continued to walk like he didn't see them coming.

As soon as the first nigga hung out the window Jay started shooting and hit him twice in the arm and chest. T-Rock and another nigga started busting with a couple fully's and Jay couldn't do shit, but duck down behind his car, but not before a hot slug shattered his collar bone.

"Ahh!" His right arm went limp and his gun clattered on the ground as it fell from his hand. He sat there up against the car feeling it rock back and forth as bullets riddled its frame. It seemed like the shooting had lasted for hours, but it was really like ten seconds. When it finally stopped Jay scrambled for his gun, crawled up into his car and headed for the hospital.

****

When Los and his crew got the call from Jay they hurried up and shot to the hospital. When they got there they went to the receptionist, found out where Jay was and went to him room. They bent the corner and there Jay was sitting on a bed with his arm in a sling and two men who were obviously detectives standing in front of him. The detectives shifted their attention to Los, Moe and Ace then back to Jay.

"Well if you remember anything here's my card." One of the DT's said as he handed Jay a card. Jay took it and nodded his head before the detectives filed out past the crew. When they left they all surrounded Jay.

"What the fuck happened?" Moe asked with his arms out by his side.

"Maaaan, I was leavin' the spot after ya'll called a nigga and shit and when I was about to get in my car them bitch ass niggas rolled up on me and started fuckin' sprayin'. They hit me, but I know for a fact I laid one of them niggas down." Jay said obviously doped up on pain killers. "Had him slumped out the window like a rag doll."

"Did you see T-Rock?" Los asked.

"It all happened so fast, I aint see nobody face, but I know it was him. I mean who the fuck else would it be?"

"So what's the damage?" Ace inquired towards the sling.

"Fuckin' bullet passed right through. It cracked my collar bone though, so I had to get a couple screws in my shit. It's a minor to a major you hear me."

"Yea well it's on with them niggas." Los said as he took a seat beside Jay.

"Oh yea, I know it. It's crunch time, so muthafuckas better start doin' they sit ups."

Chapter 5

When they left the hospital they strapped up and went on the prowl. T-Rock and his boys were nowhere to be found, so they went and shot up his dope spot. The next night T-Rock rode through and shot up the house on Wheaton, so in retaliation Los and them gave it up to T-Rock's mama house. For weeks it was a game of tennis. They went back and forth, neither side letting up for a second until one night when T-Rock was slipping.

Los was in his old school with Amaya and Magdelena. He had just picked them up from the tele and was heading home when he pulled up to a red light. He was smoking a blunt and talking shit to Amaya and Magdelena when he looked to the left and saw T-Rock and his baby mama arguing in the car in the next lane.

Los grabbed his pistol out the middle console, rolled down his window and emptied the clip. Amaya and Magdelena just sat there screaming like they were on fire. When the gun was spent Los hit the gas and ran through the red light. He flew out to Belleville to Vic's house and pounded on the door. A tall bitch that looked like Keisha off Belly answered.

"Where my bro at?"

"Who?"

"Vic. Let me in this bitch." He said as he bogarded his way inside. "Hold on muthafucka."

"Los what the hell you doin' out here? It's three in the morning." Vic asked as he entered the living room.

"Man, bro, I gotta holla at you." He said with a sense of urgency. Vic sighed then motioned for him to follow him. Los looked at Amaya and Magdelena and pointed to the couch. "I'll be right back." He said before following Vic into the kitchen. Vic went to the counter and poured himself a cup of coffee.

"You don't drink this shit, do you?"

"Naw."

"Aight now, what's goin' on?" He asked as he turned around and leaned up against the counter.

"I need to get rid of my Chevy and this." He said pulling out the gun.

"What the fuck you do?"

"Aight, you know I been into it with that nigga T-Rock. I caught him slippin' at a stop light and gave it to his bitch ass, but there was a bitch in the car too. I don't know if she got hit or not, but I know I gotta get rid of that car." Vic took a deep breath and shook his head.

"That's some dumb shit Carlos." He said pointing at his little brother.

"I was caught up in the moment." Los said shrugging.

"That's bullshit. What's wrong with you? I heard about ya'll lil beef, but what is you tryna do? Get twisted? You got everything you want and you tryna catch a fuckin' murder case. Them crackers will lock yo young ass up nigga."

"I know, but shit...... "

"You actin' like you don't. You either gone get money or play cowboy. You can't do both."

"If I wanted to hear a fuckin' sermon I woulda took my bitches to church. I came out here to see if you'd help a nigga out. I did some hot shit I know, but right now I need to get rid of this shit. You gone help me or not?"

"You know I fuckin' got you. I'm just tryna get a point across to you Lil nigga. I aint gone always be here and you got some good shit goin' on for you. Don't fuck it off over some nigga that aint worth the time. It may seem fun now, but it won't be when you sittin' in a cell doin' life."

"That won't happen."

"You don't know what the fuck gone happen. Take the F-150 and go home. Straight home and call me when you get there." Vic held his hand out and Los gave him the pistol. "The keys are hangin' up by the door."

"Thanks bro."

"Yea." When Los got home he plopped down on the couch and turned on the local news to see if he hit his target. It wasn't until the next morning when he found out that T-Rock and his baby mama were both in critical condition and the police were looking for a black Buick Regal instead of a Chevy.

Los thought that he would feel good about finally getting that nigga, but he really felt like a jack ass. For two reasons, one his baby mama didn't have shit to do with the beef, but she still got handled and two their baby was in the back seat asleep. He would have really felt like shit had the baby been hit by a stray.

Shit happened though. Everybody couldn't be the predators. After the shooting shit kind of cooled off, so Los just focused on grinding. He was going so hard that he had to take a break. July the 4th was creeping up fast, so he decided to hit up the mall with Amaya to get some shit for the World's Fair. Los was walking out of Foot Locker with a couple pairs of shoes when Amaya ran up on him smiling from ear to ear.

"Baby I just saw these ear rings over here at Jared's. I want them so bad." "How much are they?"

"Just three thousand dollars." She mumbled.

"I aint spending no fuckin' three g's on no ear rings. And you been fuckin' slackin' lately. You don't even deserve to be in the mall right now you should be flat backing somewhere."

"I need to start managing my own money then."

"Bitch, what you need to do is shut the fuck up and go sit down before I fuck you up." He handed her his bag and turned around and was met with a familiar face.

"Los? I thought that was you." Jasmine said with a warm smile. "Boy you done grown up. Look at you."

"Shit look at you." Los said checking her out. She looked like a different person with her hair short and she had gotten thicker in all the right places. They gave each other a hug and Jasmine looked over at Amaya.

"Oh hi. I'm Jasmine." She greeted with her hand out. Amaya was about to shake it, but Los looked back at her and she froze in her tracks.

"Why the fuck is you still standin' there? Go sit down." Amaya eyed him for a few secondsthen stormed off towards a vacant bench.

"Ok. That girl is way to pretty to be letting you talk to her like that. Who is that? Your girlfriend?"

"Hell naw. That bitch workin' my nerves, but what's up with you? You just upped and moved and a nigga aint seen you since."

"I moved out to Kansas City with my baby daddy."

"Baby daddy? You got a kid?"

"Yea, a little girl." She said proudly.

"That's what's up. Dude treatin' you right?"

"I wouldn't be with him if he wasn't."

"So what brings you back to the 314?"

"I came to see my family for the fourth. I'm actually glad that I ran into you."

"I know. You still want me to put it in your life, right." Jasmine busted up laughing.

"Oh, I did hear you was runnin' shit now."

"You got damn right. And a promise is a promise."

"We'll see what happens, but look, you tryin' to make some money?"

"Doin' what?"

"I got a lick back in KC. A fat lick."

"Why you don't have one of them niggas out there do that shit?" He asked suspiciously.

"Cuz I know you gone do what needs to be done. My baby daddy a square. He don't even own a gun, so askin' him aint an option."

"What you talkin' about?"

"A guaranteed hundred thousand easy. Maybe more. I've seen the cash with my own eyes. I'm telling you. This nigga so wack. It's an easy lick." Los handed her his cell phone.

"Lock your number in and Ima call you up tonight to holla at you about that shit."

"Aight baby boy." She saved her number in his phone then gave it back to him.

"Yo baby daddy down here with you?"

"Nope."

"Well, what's up then? You fuckin' with ya boy?"

"Call me later on and see." She said as she turned around and walked off. Los just stood there with a childish grin as he watched her strut.

Chapter 6

Young Hope

A couple days after the fourth Los and Ace made the trip out to Kansas City with Jasmine and her daughter. When they finally got to her house the sun had already been down for a few hours. Jasmine's daughter Christine was asleep. So she told Los and Ace to make themselves comfortable as she went and put her to bed.

Los and Ace went into the kitchen for a couple of beers and it looked like the place hadn't been cleaned in weeks. The house was nice and it was well furnished, but they could tell that Jasmine was the one who kept shit together because the kitchen was disgusting. Los went into the refrigerator and grabbed two beers when a voice from behind made him turn around.

"Who are ya'll?" A tall skinny nigga with glasses asked with two more niggas standing behind him.

"Ace." Ace said with his chest out.

"Ok Ace, what you doin' in my kitchen?"

"I'm Los, Jasmine's cousin." Los stepped in front of Ace with his hand out.

"Oh aight. Jasmine told me ya'll was comin'. He said changing his tone as he shook Los' hand.

"Where Jazzy at?"

"She just went to put Christine to bed."

"That's right. Well, I'm Meachy. These my boys Slim and Daze." He said gesturing to the niggas behind him.

"Hey baby." Jasmine greeted as she walked into the

kitchen. "I see you already met my little cousin and his friend."

"Yea. I wish you woulda told me you was comin' in tonight. I got plans to go out with my boys."

"Go have fun, I'll be here when you get back."

"I know. We just stopped over here to grab some bomb." Meachy looked at Los and Ace. "Ya'll tryna blow some of this cush?"

"Yea we can. I got some purp." They all posted up in the living room and had a little smoke session. Los was just ready to hit that lick and get back home. Meachy and his dudes were aight, but they were different than a muthafucka. They threw their blunts at each other instead of passing the shit then they'd cuz each other and turn right back around and call each other dog. Then on top of that Jasmine had already let him know that her baby daddy wasn't about the business, so Los and Ace really weren't feeling him.

When they finally left it was around ten o'clock and Los was feeling antsy. It was the first time he had been out of St. Louis since he was fifteen and he was ready to get back. He pushed up on Jasmine who had started trying to clean the kitchen.

"What up? We gone do this shit or what?" He asked as he dropped his empty bottle in the trash.

"Tomorrow night."

"Tomorrow? What the fuck is so special about tomorrow?"
"I just got home. Can't I relax and get some rest?"

"You on some bullshit Jazz. I got shit to do."

"Like what? If I was on some bullshit I wouldn't have had you come way out here." She walked up to him, took his hands and put them on her ass. "Just relax Lil daddy. I got you." Los leaned in to kiss her, but she held up her index finger to his lips. "You gone have to wait for that."

"I knew you was on some bullshit." Los said as he pulled away from her and headed back into the living room.

"You gone help me clean this kitchen?"

"Fuck your kitchen." He replied over his shoulder. He went and plopped down on the couch next to Ace.

"So what's up?"

"She talkin' bout tomorrow night." Ace let out a sigh of relief.

"Good. I'm tired than a muthafucka." Ace said as he yawned.

"Take yo ass to sleep then nigga." Los stated dismissively. Ace scooted down to the other side of the couch and stretched out while Los just sat there texting on his phone. Ten minutes later Jasmine walked into the room smiling. "What the fuck so funny?"

"Aw you mad at me?" She asked as she sat down next to him. "Who you textin'?"

"Don't worry about it." Jasmine looked over her shoulder to make sure Ace was asleep before scooting in close to Los. She leaned in and gave him a kiss.

"You really think I got you out here on some bullshit, don't you?" She asked looking him in the eyes.

"Hell yea I do. I aint come out here to meet ya nigga and sleep on your couch. I came out here to get paid."

"That's it? That's all you came for?"

"What else is there?" He asked like he didn't know where the situation was going.

"You sho right nigga." Jasmine stood up like she had an attitude, but Los grabbed her wrist and pulled her into his lap. He took his pistol out of his pocket and sat it down next to him. Los eased his hand into her pants and started to massage her clit as their lips met again. All he could think about was what types of positions he was going to have her in. He had been wanting a piece of that ass for a long time and he was finally about to get his shot.

Jasmine pulled his hand out of her panties and sucked on his finger as she straddled his lap. She had his dick standing at attention and he was ready to put the swipe game down. Los pulled Jasmine's shirt off and began to kiss her neck and breasts as he went for the bra strap. When he got it unhooked her perfect brown nipples popped out like a jack in the box. Los went to work on them like he was a newborn baby.

Jasmine let out little soft moans while she fondled with Los' belt that drove him crazy. He palmed her ass and was about to stand up with her when they heard somebody unlocking the door. Jasmine looked at Los with wide eyes and in one smooth motion she hopped up, snatched her shirt and bra from the couch and ran to her room. Los slid his pistol in between the couch pillows so Meachy wouldn't see it and acted like he was still texting. When Meachy walked in he nodded at Los.

"What up wit it cuz?"

"What up?" Los replied without looking up from his phone.

"Where Jazzy at?" He asked as he locked the door.

"I think she went to sleep already."

"Oh. Aight. Well, Ima holla at you in the morning then dog."

"Yea, its on." Los said light weight salty. The next day went by slow as hell. Ace and Los had to put up with Meachy and his off brand ass homeboys the whole time. Los couldn't understand why Jasmine even fucked with the clown. He was the epitome of a square. He was a video game tester and anything street related was a foreign subject to him. One thing was for sure, he knew that Los and Jasmine's weren't cousins because every time they interacted with each other he watched like a hawk.

When nightfall came Los was happy as hell. Him and Ace said their goodbyes to Meachy and his boys and they rode out. Jasmine took Meachy's car and Los and Ace followed her to a white two story house. Jasmine had already run down the details of the lick to them. The house was a dope house slash gambling shack and the nigga that ran it only dealt with big money. A nigga couldn't come in and shoot dice or play cards unless he started off with at least five grand.

The dude that ran the shack was an old trick. That's how Jasmine found out how vulnerable he was. He was trying to buy some pussy and let her know where he kept all of the money. There was always at least twenty grand active in the dice game and even more stashed in the floor underneath where the old trick nigga sat.

Jasmine went in first and made a couple petty side bets on the dice game while . scoping the place out. She flirted with the trick nigga and texted Los letting him know that there were five people inside, including her. Los and Ace got out of the car and casually strolled into the house. As soon as they walked through the door they pulled their guns out and Jasmine started screaming.

"Ahhh! Oh my God don't shoot me!"

"Shut up bitch." Los grabbed her by her hair and threw her to the floor.

"What the fuck is this?!" The trick asked as he stood up.

"A fuckin' robbery nigga. Fuck it look like?" Ace growled as he ran up on him. Los cleaned off the pool table they had been shooting dice on and started making the three niggas empty their pockets. He put everything into his back pack and turned his gun on the trick.

"Where the rest of it at?"

"That's everything."

"Nooooo!!" Jasmine screamed making Los look at the three niggas he had just relieved of their stacks. He saw the glint of a chrome pistol and with lightning speed he turned his gun on the nigga and let off two shots. They both hit him in the chest and he fell to the floor bleeding like a stuck pig. Los turned his cannon on the other two niggas.

"Try something slick and you gone be layin' down there next to him." By then Ace had been rummaging around the pool table and had stumbled across the hidden compartment in the floor.

"What's this?" He asked with a smile as he bent down and pulled up the piece of wood. "Jackpot!" Ace exclaimed. Los looked over Ace's shoulder and saw all those stacks and started cheesing from ear to ear. The trick just stood there with his hands up seething, as Ace loaded up his bag.

"Ya'll gone fuckin' pay for this." He said under his breath.

"What is that? A threat?" Los asked incredulously. The trick got some balls and dropped his hands.

"Take it how you wanna take it lil nigga!" Los looked at him like 'nigga please' before pumping a single bullet into his abdomen. "Ahhhh!" The trick fell back into the corner holding his gut.

"That tough shit won't get you no where pimpin'."

"Yo I got it. Let's roll!" Ace said as he threw his bag on his back and headed for the door. Los backed out of the house and blew a kiss to Jasmine before taking off towards the car. They hopped in and burnt rubber. Five minutes later Jasmine called and had them meet her at a Motel 8 right off the highway. When they got there she was standing outside room 218 smoking a cigarette.

They went into the room, Jasmine closed and locked the door and they dumped everything out on the bed. Jasmine put her cigarette out in the ash tray then punched Los in the chest.

"Nigga you aint have to grab my hair like that."

"I had to make that shit look good. I appreciate that heads up though. If it wasn't for you dude probably would have got off at a nigga."

"Didn't I tell you I got you lil nigga." They all sat down and counted up all the money. It all came to one hundred and thirty thousand dollars. Los was geeked up. He already knew what he was going to do with his cut.

"Even though this was really my lick Ima take the thirty aight. So aint no discrepancies." Jasmine said as she loaded her money into one of the bags.

"You sure?" Ace asked.

"Ya'll did the dirty work. I just set it up. Just don't go and blow that shit or Ima be mad." She joked.

"So when you gone come out to the Lou and fuck with a nigga? We gotta finish what we started."

"You got my number, just stay in touch, we'll figure something out."

"Yea aight." Los looked at Ace. "You ready to hit that highway my nigga?"

"Ready when you are." He said as he closed the bag up.

"I guess this is it."

"Yea for now." Jasmine gave Los a hug and a kiss then walked over and gave Ace a hug. "I'm about to go check out of this room. Ya'll do me a favor and follow me home."

"We got you." Los and Ace got into the whip and listened to 50 Cents "Ski Mask Way" as Jasmine handled her business. They followed her back to her house to make sure she made it there safely then hit the highway heading back to the 314.

Chapter 7

When Los got home he was tired as hell, but he was in a good mood. It was about four in the morning so he figured he'd get a couple hours of sleep in before he got out and handled his business. Los went into the basement expecting to see Amaya and Magdelena in bed, but he only saw Magdelena. He dropped his bag on the floor and when he sat down Magdalena's eyes slowly fluttered open.

"Hey Papi. I missed you." She sat up and tried to kiss him, but he palmed her face and pushed it away.

"Bitch, is you crazy? What I tell you about all that kissin' shit."

"Sorry, I just missed you so much."

"Where Amaya at?" He asked as he kicked his shoes off. "Um. Amaya got arrested the night you left."

"What? For what?" Los stood up and turned the lights on.

"I think trafficking. She got caught with some coke."

"Why the fuck you aint bond her out? Why you aint call me you stupid bitch?"

"I don't know." Magdelena broke down crying and Los couldn't do shit but shake his head.

"Get the fuck out my house and don't come back till you got five grand."

"But Papi. ...." Los grabbed her arm and drug her naked body out of the bed onto the floor.

"Don't fuckin' make me repeat myself." He said before walking over to his computer desk. He looked through the phone book and found the number to the county. He found out that Amaya was being held on possession charges and her bond was twenty thousand dollars. The next thing he did was find a twenty four hour bail bondsman. He had the man meet him at the county where Los paid him the two g's in cash and at 6: 10 am Amaya was walking through the doors.

"You couldn't make it one day without me, huh?" He scolded her making her put her head down. "What happened Amaya?"

"I was trying to surprise you when you came back."

"By doin' what?" He asked as they walked to the Lexus. "Shit this is a surprise."

"I almost sold nine ounces. I only had like a half left, but the police came in so I ran to the bathroom and flushed that. I forgot about a couple grams of coke I had in my purse. They found it and booked me." She explained as she got into the car.

"Where were you?"

"At the funky ass Scottish Inn. I knew you were mad at me when you left. I was just trying to make you happy."

"So where the money at?"

"At the house in one of my shoe boxes. It should be about ten grand."

"You made ten racks in one day?" Los asked in disbelief.

"Almost. So many people were coming through and it scared the shit out of me. I'm glad I went home and put the money up." Los grabbed the back of her neck and kissed her on the forehead.

"That's why I love you lil mama."

"I love you too." She replied cheesing from ear to ear.

****

When Los got home he rolled up a blunt, dumped all the money he had saved up, including the lick money and the doe Amaya hustled up, on the bed and started counting. After about forty five minutes, another blunt and a few hand cramps, Los counted all of his money and it came out to be one hundred and forty one thousand dollars.

Los loaded the forty one g's in his Louie bag then put the rest of the money up. He hopped into the Lexus and headed downtown to the dealership that he bought it from. He parked, got out and went inside to see what was on the showroom floor. The same black man that sold him the Lex met him in the middle of the floor with a big smile and a handshake.

"Back already? What can I help you with this time?"

"I don't know yet." Los said as he looked around. "I'm

tryna trade in that Lexus for something else." The sales man pointed to a lime green Lamborghini.

"How about the Lambo? This is the new LP670-4 Super Veloce. It has a 6.5 liter V-12, tops out at 209 miles per hour and can go from zero to sixty in 3.2 seconds. There's only 350 of these cars world wide, so if you want something nobody else will have, this would be the perfect choice."

"Naw, I aint diggin' that color. It's too loud man."

"I could refer you to a body shop right up the street. The owner's a good friend of mine and I could make sure he takes care of you." Los shook his head. A Lamb would definitely turn heads and that's what Los wanted, but a lime green Lamborghini would attract way too much attention, especially in Los' neighborhood. He looked around for a few seconds until he spotted something that fit his personality.

"What's up with that one?" Los asked pointing to a black Jaguar sedan.

"That's a beautiful car, isn't it? That's the Jaguar XFR. It has a 5 liter V-8 and it isn't as fast as the Lamborghini, but it's guaranteed to leave all of the competition in the dust."

"How much is it?"

"Eighty thousand." Los walked around to the driver side and got inside the car. He put his hands on the steering wheel and then adjusted the seat before stepping out and tossing the keys to the Lexus to the salesman.

"Handle that paperwork. I'm takin' this one home."

"Good choice man. I'm on it." Thirty minutes later Los drove his Jaguar off the showroom floor. He had to pay twenty thousand to make up the difference and with the twenty one he had left he decided to take the Jag to the body shop the salesman had recommended. He picked out a set of twenty tow inch rims and a sound system that came to twelve g's. They told him that they'd be finished when the car in about an hour and a half so Los left and headed for a little cafe around the corner from the shop.

When he walked in he instantly spotted Ever Since sitting over in the far corner with two white men in suits. Los pulled his fitted cap low over his face as he ordered a couple donuts and an orange juice. He sat at the counter and kept his eyes glued to that corner. Los didn't want to jump to conclusions, but it looked like Ever Since was talking to the Feds.

Los took out his cell phone, held I up like he was trying to get some reception and took a picture of them. A couple seconds later one of the men in suits walked over to the counter. He ordered a bagel and when he pulled out his walled to pay for the shit Los saw a glimpse of his badge. Los snatched up his bottle of orange juice and left the cafe, He walked across the street to an internet cafe and took a seat at the window. He watched until he saw the suits leave then he headed outside, walked to the end of the block, crossed the street then went back towards the cafe Ever Since was in. As if on cue when Los walked past the door Ever Since came out.

He stopped dead in his tracks and his mouth instantly got dry.

"Los? What you doin' down here boy?" He

asked nervously making Los turn around.

"Aw shit. What up my nigga?" Los smiled and shook Ever Since's hand. "I got my car in the shop so I got a couple hours to burn. What you got goin' on?"

"Not too much." He lied shaking his head. "Getting' some coffee and shit."

"Huh. You drove way down here just to get some coffee?" Los probed.

"They got the best coffee in the city plus I been tryna get at lil mama."

"The white girl behind the counter?"

"Yea, but actually she's Russian." Los shrugged his shoulders.

"A pecker wood is a pecker wood to me my nigga. But look I'm finna go check on my car man, so I guess I'll catch up with you later."

"Yea. You should call a nigga so we can chop it up. I aint seen you in a minute."

"Aight. When I get some time we'll do that." Los said thinking. "Yea right. You aint about to set me up." "It's on though, my nigga." They shook hands and Los walked off heading for the detail shop. On the walk to the shop Los thought about how he could tell Vic. He didn't want to call because the phones might have been tapped and if the Feds were watching Vic, he damn sure wasn't going to drive over there in a brand new Jaguar bought with drug proceeds.

Los started going through his phone book looking for somebody to pick him up and take him to Vic's house. He highlighted Denise's number and pressed talk. She was perfect because she was the only legal person he knew. He just hoped

So that she was in town because after high school she went off to attend college at Missou and rarely came back. After a few rings she answered sounding groggy.

"Hello."

"What's up baby girl. This Carlos."

"Oh, hey what's up."

"I didn't mean to wake you up."

"It's ok. I guess it's time for me to start my day."

"You at school?"

"No, I'm at my mother's house. I'm leaving tomorrow. Why what's up?"

"I need you to do me a favor, come pick me up and take me to my bro's house in Belleville."

"And what's wrong with you car?"

"It's in the shop. That's where I'm at right now."

Denise sighed.

"I guess. Let me get myself together and I'll come get you."

"You know I love you right?"

"Mmhmmm. I'll call you when I'm on my way." She hung up and Los went into the shop to see Marcus, the shop's owner, hooking up the sound system. The rims were glistening and Los couldn't help but to smile.

"How much longer you think it's gone be?"

"Probably another hour. I know that aint what I told you earlier, but trust me it'll be worth the wait."

"Aight man. I'm trustin' you wit my baby. When ya'll close?"

"Five, why you leavin'?" He asked wiping the sweat from his brow with a handkerchief.

"Yea, I got some business to handle."

"Well do ya thing pimpin'. If you come after five just call me and I'll open the shop up for you."

"Bet that." Los went and sat in the reception area and waited for Denise. When she called he gave her directions and twenty minutes later she was walking through the door of the auto shop. Everybody stopped and stared as she strutted into the building. Los hadn't seen her in a minute and she had always been a cutie, but she walked upon him looking like Esther Baxter's little sister. He stood up and smiled making it obvious that he was gawking.

"Damn girl when you get body like that?".

"Shut up." She said playfully as they hugged. "Where's the Lexus?" She asked as she looked around. Los pointed across the garage to the Jag.

"Damn. That's how you pushin'?"

"Just copped it this morning." He bragged.

"You doin' too much."

"Naw, I aint doin' enough. I'm still trippin' off you. You lookin' good D."

"Thank you. You aint lookin' too shabby yourself."

"Yea, I know." Denise playfully hit him in the arm.

"Well are you ready to go?"

"Yea, come on." Los chunked up the deuces to Marcus as they left and got into Denise's Chevy Malibu. They rode out to Belleville chopping it up and catching up on each other's lives. All of a sudden Los was thinking about fucking Denise. Ace wouldn't like that shit one bit and because of that Los always use to blow her off. Real homeboys were hard to come by and Los didn't want to ruin his friendship with Ace over some pussy.

When they got to Vic's house Denise pulled up into the driveway and parked behind Vic's F-150. They got out, knocked on the door a couple times and Vic answered looking real dapper. He was rocking some square toe snake skin shoes, slacks, a button down shirt and a pair of Louie Vuitton shades. He looked surprised to see Los standing there.

"What up lil nigga? What you doin' out here?" He looked at Denise and lifted his shades. "And who is this beautiful young woman right here."

"Nigga that's Denise. Ace lil sister." Los answered like he had asked the dumbest question imaginable.

"Oh." He said with a bald fist up to his mouth. "Damn lil mama."

"Hi to you too Vic." She said cheesing.

"Damn nigga you gone let us in?" Vic stepped to the side allowing them to enter the house.

"You kinda caught me at a bad time. I got shit to do."

"Well that shit gone have to wait cuz I gotta fuckin' holla at you."

"What you done did now?"

"I aint do shit." Los looked at Denise. "Gone head and post up for a minute D. I gotta talk to this nigga."

"Ya'll do ya thing." She said as she took a seat on the couch. "You want something to drink?" Vic asked.

"I'm fine. Handle ya'll business."

"Don't be bashful. If you need something help yourself." They walked into the kitchen and Vic got right to the point. "So what the hell is so important?" Los handed Vic his phone and let him see the picture he took at the cafe, Vic looked at him with a confused look on his face. "What the fuck is this?"

"That's Ever Since talkin' to the fuckin' Feds." Los

said pointing to the phone. "What?"
"That's Ever Since talkin' to the Feds." He repeated.

"I fuckin' heard you nigga. How you know they Feds? Where this picture come from?"

"Aight check this out. I took my car to the shop this morning and while they was workin' on it I hit up that cafe they in. I saw Ever Since talkin' to them clowns and I took a picture of that shit."

"How you know they Feds?"

"One of em bought something while I was at the counter and I saw his fuckin' badge. I'm telling you, they Feds bro. I fuckin' seen it with my own eyes. That nigga Ever Since gotta be telling."

"Did he see you?" Vic asked as he took a seat at the table.

"Yea, after the fact I pushed up on him. I didn't say nothing though. I played it smart."

"I can't fuckin' believe this shit." Vic said rubbing his face. "So what you want me to do?"

"Nothin'. Ima take care of it."

"Bullshit." He objected. "I found him out so it's only right that I do the nigga. I aint even have to tell you. I coulda just handled his bitch ass then told you after the fact." Vic just sat there staring out into space thinking. After about a full minute of silence Vic finally looked up at Los.

"Aight. Don't say nothing to nobody, especially your

crew. The last thing we need is muthafuckas panicking. Just keep your phone on, Ima call you tonight."

"Bet that. I'm finna go home and crash. I aint slept in two days."

"Fuck you been doin'?"

"A whole lot of nothing." Vic stood up and hugged Los, then pulled away from him and pointed at him.

"Stay outta shit lil nigga. We gone take care of this nigga then everybody need to take a trip somewhere. Just stay off the radar aight."

"Aight." He said before leaving with Denise. When they arrived at the detail shop they said their goodbyes to each other and when Denise went to give him a hug Los kissed her. She pulled back and looked at him.

"I'm sorry. I don't know what I was thinking."

"Don't be. You know I use to have a major league crush on you back in high school, right?"

"Yea I knew, but I shit, your brother is my best friend." Denise leaned in and kissed him.

"And.... " She said before kissing him again.. "I'm grown. He doesn't need to approve who I fuck with."

"Yea well...... "

"I'm going back to school in the morning Los. Aint no telling the next time I'm coming back so if you want to you can call me tonight. I would really like you to, but the choice is yours."

"I'll see what's up." She leaned over the middle console again and began to kiss him passionately. When she pulled away from him she looked at him and smiled.

"You do that." Los got out of the car and watched it disappear up the street before going inside the shop and getting his Jag. He jumped into his whip, went home and got some sleep.

Chapter 8

"You aint never seen them pies/I'm talkin' so much white it'll hurt ya eyes/I really lived it man/Countin' so much paper it'll hurt your hands/Let's get it." Los' ring tone woke him up from dream land. He sat up in bed wiping the sleep from his eyes with one hand and blindly searched the covers for his phone with the other. When he found it, he pressed talk and put it up to his ear.

"Yea?"

"You still sleep?" Vic asked in a serious tone. "Yea. What time is it?"

"Eight thirty. Get your ass up and meet me at my old spot in thirty minutes."

"It's on." Los hung up, snatched some shit out of his closet and went upstairs to take a quick shower. He saw Amaya, Magdalena and Jay sitting on the couch as he passed through the living room.

"Hey daddy. I see you finally got up." Amaya said with a big smile, but Los ignored her and grilled Magdalena.

"Bitch, I know you got that money or you wouldn't be sittin' on my couch."

"Yea Papi. It's on your nightstand. I didn't want to wake you up."

"Go get it and bring it to me." Without hesitation Magdalena stood up and ran to the basement. Los went and took a shower and when he got out the five g's was sitting on the counter. He took it, went into the basement and got dressed. He tucked his pistol into his jeans and went back upstairs.

"Aye Jay let me use the MC."

"Where you goin'?" He asked as he pulled the keys out of his pocket. "I'll holla at you about it later on."

"It's on my nigga. Stay safe out there." He said as he handed Los the keys.

"Always." Los left, hopped in the Monte Carlo and headed to Vic's old spot. As soon as he turned the block he saw a black old school parked in the driveway. Vic turned over the ignition and backed out of the driveway and Los just followed. They rode out to Charlie Park in East St. Louis where T-Ko stayed. In front of his house was his burgundy Suburban and Ever Since's silver Cadillac CTS. Los and Vic pulled up, parked and went into the house to see Ever Since, T-Ko and O sitting on the couch smoking and playing PS3. Ever Since looked up at them with a nervous grin on his face.

"What up Los. I was just telling these niggas how I ran into you downtown this morning." He said as he ashed the blunt in the ash tray.

"Oh yea?" Los pulled out his cell phone, found the picture and handed it to Ever Since. "You tell em who you was downtown meetin'?" All the blood drained from his face and his stomach dropped as he tried to think of something to say.

"How long you been compromised nigga?" Vic asked as he took a seat on the coffee table right in front of Ever Since. He couldn't say a word because his mouth was so dry. His heart was beating so hard that he could hear it in his head. He felt it. It was like it was going to leap from his chest. Vic took a deep breath. "How long you been snitchin'?"

"Man. Vic it aint like that. ..... " Vic slapped him in his mouth.

"How is it then? Explain to me how it is that you can turn on your family and work with the Feds."

"Vic." He looked at everybody then back at Vic. "They, they caught me red handed with two thangs man. They was tryna railroad me man. It was in my bitch car so they was tryna charge both of us unless I cooperated. I just couldn't let her go down for that shit bro. You gotta understand." Los lashed out and socked Ever Since right in his jaw knocking him from his seat.

"Vic aint your fuckin' brother nigga!" Vic held up a hand signaling Los to calm down. He looked down at Ever Since and took another deep breath.

"Ok. We have the why, now when did this happen?"

"About two months ago." Vic started laughing.

"So that's why you was askin' me questions about the connect?"

"They said they'd pass right over us if I could give them the plug."

"Oh, so you was tryna look out for us, huh?"

"Vic man .... " Vic held up his index finger to his lips instantly silencing Ever

Since.

"How much do they know?" Ever Since closed his eyes and exhaled, "Latrell, answer my got damn question."

"They know that you're in charge and that you're the only one that knows who the plug is. That's it."

"That's it?" Vic asked sarcastically. He stood up and football kicked Ever Since's face. The sound was disgusting. T-Ko jumped up from the couch with his pistol drawn.

"You betta swallow that shit. If you get some blood on my carpet Ima fuckin' kill you!" He said with his gun pointed at Ever Since's head. Ever Since rolled over onto his back and struggled to swallow the blood and teeth that filled his mouth. Vic held out his hand and helped Ever Since up.

"You know what comes next. But you still have a choice. Either accept it and take it like a man so we can get it over with quick and easy or try to fight and we make it slow and painful. It's up to you." Ever Since dropped his head and started crying.

"I' m so sorry ya'll I, I.. "

"Save that shit for somebody who cares." O interjected as he got to his feet. "That's what got you into this shit in the first place. You don't know how to keep your fuckin' mouth closed."

"So what's it gonna be?"

"Let's get it over with man." He said quietly. They all filed out of the house and with Ever Since, Vic got into his old school and Los followed in the MC. They went to a secluded spot in the woods way out in Cape Cod. They made Ever Since get into the trunk of his own car and Vic handed Los a chrome 357.

"Do the honors." Los took the gun, aimed it at Ever Since's head and pulled the trigger twice. His head splattered all over the trunk and his lifeless body just laid there in an awkward position. Vic nodded towards the car and T-Ko and 0 doused the trunk in gasoline. Vic lit a match and dropped it into the trunk before closing it up. He took the gun from Los and tucked it into his pocket.

"You good on work?"

"I'm straight bro."

"Good. We shakin' for a few weeks aight. I'll be in touch." "It's on bro. Love you my nigga."

"Love you too." Vic, T-Ko and 0 hopped in Vic's car and Los got into Jay's Monte Carlo. He rode the whole way back to St. Louis in complete silence. He couldn't shake the picture of Ever Since's eyes from his mind. Los looked down at his phone and saw that it was going on one o'clock. He debated it for a few minutes then he finally caved in and called Denise. She picked up after two rings.

"What do you want?" She answered with an attitude.

"You told me to call you."

"So you wait until one in the morning? What, was I the last resort or something."

"You know it aint nothing like that. I just had some business I had to take care of that was real important."

"Yea right."

"For real Denise. I'm tryin' to fuck with you. I'm on the highway right now."

"If you're serious then I'll be right here waiting on you."

"I'm on my way."

"When you get here park up the street and come around to my window."

"What are we, twelve?"

"Just do it. I don't want my mama to wake up."

"It's on. Give me a minute, I'll be there." When Los got to Li-City he stopped at a 7-11, bought some condoms and shot over to Denise's. Just like she said he parked up the street and walked around the back of the house and knocked on her window. Denise peeked out the blinds before opening it up. "Why you aint just open up the front door?"

"Just go with it. You gone stand out there all night or are you coming in?"

"Move." Denise got out of the way and Los climbed in through the window feeling like a little kid.

"Look at you sneakin' in my window in the middle of the night." She joked as she locked the bedroom door.

"We coulda just went and got a room or something." Los said closing the window.

"I don't see any fun in that." She said as she walked up on him. "Don't forget that my mama's in the other room, so we'll have to be extra quiet."

"Practice what you preach." He said before pulling her close and kissing her. They didn't waste any time, they instantly started tearing each other's clothes off. Denise laid back on the bed and opened her legs as Los put the condom on. Los never broke eye contact with her as he climbed on the bed and mounted her. Denise just laid there breathing heavily as he kissed the nape of her neck. He reached down and guided himself in and she tried to scoot away as he fully penetrated her tight passage.

"Uhh. Los you feel so good." She moaned softly in his ear as he long dicked her, pulling it out to the tip and running it all the way up in her. She had some fire in the hole and Los knew that if he would have fucked her back in high school like he wanted to she would have had his young ass twisted. "Let me get on top." She said almost breathless.

Los pulled out and laid on his back. He watched intently as she grabbed his swipe and slowly slid down on it. Los explored her body with his hands as she gyrated her hips on his manhood, and rode him like a four wheeler. Los palmed her ass and began to thrust upward making her scream out in pleasure.

"Shhhh! That was loud." He said in between thrusts."

"J. ....J ..... .Just keep doin' what you're doin'." Denise said as she leaned forward and put her face in the pillows. She tried to meet Los thrust for thrust, but it was too much for her. "Ahhhh!" She screamed into the pillow as her legs began to shake uncontrollably. Denise had an explosive orgasm that rocked her whole body making her go limp, but Los continued to pound away at it like Tyson in his prime.

Los flipped her over onto her back and stayed at it until he felt himself about to bust one. He couldn't even enjoy the big moment because just as he came he felt the condom break.

"Wicked." He quickly pulled out and pulled what was left of the condom off. "What?"

"The fuckin' condom broke!"

"It doesn't matter. I'm on birth control, so I can't get pregnant." Denise started laughing at him. "You should see your face."

"Fuck you." Los relaxed and laid down next to her.

"You aint had enough yet?" She asked playfully as she laid her head on his chest.

"Give me a couple minutes. I got something for your ass." Round town never happened because a few minutes later they were both out cold.

Chapter 9

Los woke up around six the next morning and had sex with Denise again before sneaking back out of the window. He had forgotten his problems for that night, but as soon as he got into Jay's Monte Carlo reality struck him. He had shot niggas before and he like how it felt to get at shit, but he had never actually killed anyone. And then the nigga he killed was one of the niggas he looked up to in the game.

He just couldn't believe that Ever Since was snitching. It had him feeling like if that nigga could flip anybody could. All of a sudden Los was wondering if he could trust his crew. He wanted to believe that he could, but there was really no telling. Los just shrugged it off, went home and took a shower. He shouldn't spend every waking moment thinking about that shit.

All three of them were sitting on the couch when Los walked through the door. He dropped the keys to the Monte Carlo on the table and headed for the kitchen without even acknowledging their presence. Ace stood up and followed him into the kitchen.

"Say Los, what the fuck is goin' on with you man? You been actin' weird ever since we got back from KC." Los went into the refrigerator, grabbed a beer, popped the top and took a sip before even looking at Ace. "You aight?" Los just shrugged his shoulders and shook his head. "Did you know the police found Ever Since out in the woods somewhere? They said he was shot and set on fire." Los took another sip of beer before responding.

"Yea. He was a snitch." He said blandly.

"You fuckin' serious?"

"As a heart attack."

"That's fucked up. You know T-Rock out the hospital. I heard he got a shit bag and his baby mama still in critical condition. Just so you know. Niggas gone have to be on point."

"Pst. I stay on point nigga."

"I'm just sayin' I don't know what the fuck your problem is, but you aint gotta act like that with me nigga. I'm on your side muthafucka. Remember that shit." Ace said before walking out of the kitchen.

****

Jacco was a short dark skinned nigga with major mental issues. He was only twenty, but he had already done seven years in various correctional facilities, been shot five times and stabbed twice. When he finally got released his first cousin T-Roc k was just getting out of the hospital.

When he saw his little cousin he went ballistic. T-Rock was pale and skinny looking like a crack head that had went through chemotherapy. But what really sent Jacco over the edge was when he saw the colostomy bag T-Rock had to carry around with him everywhere.

"So what up lil cuz? What you tryna do?" Jacco asked as he puffed on a Newport dipped in water. T-Rock just shook his head.

"Nothin' yet." He answered in a low raspy voice. He sat at his mother's dining room table with a plate full of food in front of him. She was basically forcing him to eat in an attempt to get his weight and strength back up. "I gotta go visit baby later on. I hate that she's still in that fuckin' place and I'm out here."

"That's cuz God want you to handle that pussy ass nigga that did this shit. I hear that that Lil' faggot drivin' around in a got damn Jaguar. We need to lay him the fuck down and hit his pockets."

"Believe me. That nigga time comin'. I just......... look promise me that you aint gone do shit till I get ready to. I don't want nothing to happen to that nigga unless I'm involved in it."

"How Ima promise some shit like that?" He asked as he took another pull from the cigarette.

"Fuckin' promise me got damnit!" T-Rock growled as he grabbed hold of Jacco's shirt. "That nigga's mine. If you touch him Ima fuckin' kill you."

"Aight cuz. You got it. Damn." T-Rock let him go then turned in his seat and began to eat.

Chapter 10

After Ace told Los that T-Rock had been released from the hospital he went on alert. He kept a finger on the trigger and his eyes in the rearview mirror when he was in traffic. But after a few weeks passed and T-Rock never surfaced Los dropped his guard. He figured that the nigga had learned his lesson and didn't want anymore problems, so Los dismissed him as a threat and went on about his business.

When Vic got back into town Los hit him up, copped two birds and it was as if everything was back to normal. He just didn't know how wrong he was. The money was rolling in and it was like his hoes were working over time. Shit was just going Los' way and even though he had been in the streets doing his thing he didn't have enough experience to recognize the calm period before the storm.

Los had just walked into the spot carrying his Louie bag with eighteen ounces of soft in it. He pulled a bag of dro out of his pocket and tossed it to Moe who was sitting on the couch counting his money.

"Here roll that shit up."

"It's on." Moe dumped the weed on the coffee table as Los went into the kitchen with his bag. He dropped it on the counter, went into the cabinet and pulled out a little electrical scale, a Pyrex pot and some baking soda. He put it all on the counter next to his bag before going back into the living room.

"Where Magdalena at? She here yet?"

"Yea, she in the bathroom my nigga." Moe said as two smokers walked in. "What ya'll need?" Los heard Moe ask as he headed for the bathroom. Los knocked twice then opened the door and stood there dumbfounded.

"Bitch what the fuck is you doin'?!"

"Papi, wait." Los back handed her in the mouth then grabbed her by the hair and punched her in the stomach making her double over and drop the strait shooter and butane lighter she had in her hands.

"How long you been fuckin' smoking crack, bitch?"

"I....I....." Los slapped her again busting her lip. "Papi, noooooo! Stop please." She screamed as two more slaps met her face setting her cheeks on fire.

"Is you fuckin' stupid or something?" Los pushed her back and she fell into the tub. He reached down, picked up the broken strait shooter and threw it at her. Moe came and stuck his head in the door.

"What's goin' on?"

"This stupid bitch is a fuckin' crack head." He said disdainfully. She just sat there in the bath tub scared to move.

"Damn lil mama, you goin' out like that?" Moe started laughing.

"Get yo dumb ass up and go in the kitchen." Los told her before walking out past Moe. He went into the kitchen and pulled the eighteen ounces of work out of his bag, along with a pint of VSOP. Magdalena slowly entered the kitchen as Los weighed out 126 grams of soft and dumped it into the Pyrex pot. He poured some of the VSOP into the pot then weighed out 31 grams of baking soda and added it to the mix.

Los threw that shit in the microwave and watched it closely, pulling it out ever so often to hit it with the egg beater. When he felt like it was ready he threw a tray of ice in the mix turning it into a hard beige cookie. He sat it off to the side, grabbed another Pyrex pot and repeated the process again. When he started on the third batch he looked back at Magdalena and shook his head.

"You're fuckin' pathetic."

"Papi, I'm sorry. I haven't been doing it long. I promise I can stop....."

"Shut the fuck up. You prolly been smoking the whole time." He said as he turned back to the counter and began to weigh out the dope. "I specifically told ya'll bitches not to smoke that shit. I aint even want ya'll snortin' this shit cuz I fuckin' knew this would happen. Now you useless to me. I don't need no fuckin' crack head bitch."

"Noooooo!!" Magdalena screamed before two consecutive gun shots went off. Los instantly went for the gun on his hip, but a hot slug ripped through his back spinning him around and making him drop his burner. It clattered on the tile floor as Los fell back against the counter. He locked eyes with T-Rock before two flashes of light sent him into darkness.

T-Rock tucked his pistol then ran over to the counter and threw all the dope, Pyrex pots and all in the Louie bag. He threw it on his back, looked down and kicked Los' limped body.

"I told you I'd take your shit nigga!" He spat.

"Yo T-Rock, let's shake!!" Jacco yelled from the living room. T-Rock casually strolled out of the kitchen, but not before catching a glimpse of Magdalena who as slumped over in the corner with half of her head missing. What a waste of pussy. "Hurry the fuck up nigga!"

"Here I come." T-Rock broke into a sprint and ran out of the house with Jacco and his other two goons. They jumped into the Mazda that was waiting in front of the house for them and burned out just as Ace pulled up with Amaya.

"Yo Maya go see what happened. I'm finna follow these niggas." Amaya quickly got out of the car and ran into the house as Ace smashed after the Mazda. As soon as she walked in the front door she saw Moe sitting on the couch covered in blood. His head was tilted to the side, and his mouth and eyes were wide open. Amaya just stood there with her hands to her mouth as her eyes watered up.

"Carlos! Baby where are you?" She yelled as she ran to the back of the house. She checked the bedrooms and the bathroom and came up empty, but when she• hit the kitchen she almost threw up. There was so much blood that it looked unreal. Like a scene out of a horror movie. She ran over to Los and cradled his head. "Oh my God baby please be alive. Please be alive." Amaya held her fingers underneath his nose and was relieved to see that he was still breathing, but barely.

She pulled her cell phone out and called 911.

****

Ace punched it in his Lexus and quickly caught up

with the raggedy ass Mazda. Even though it was dark he saw the passenger and instantly knew who it was. He saw how those niggas piled into the car and burnt rubber. They had to have been on some ill shit and all of a sudden Ace started thinking the worst for his homies.

Ace floored the accelerator till he got right up on the Mazda then put it on cruise control. He swerved on the right side of the car, rolled down his window and emptied the clip into the passenger side. When his gun was spent he took the car off of cruise control and punched the accelerator again, but not before somebody hung out the window and started busting back.

All Ace heard was the pings of the hot slugs tearing up his cars frame. He hit the brakes and a stray bullet passed through the Lexus and hit Ace right in the head. He was so caught up in the moment that he didn't even notice. Ace just turned the car around and he headed back for the trap house. When he got there he saw the same thing Amaya had seen just minutes earlier.

"Fuck!!" He yelled swinging at the air. "Amaya!"

"I'm in the kitchen." Ace slowly walked into the kitchen afraid of what he might see. A lump formed in his throat when he saw Amaya sitting there with Los' head in her lap. Amaya looked up at him and her blood shot red eyes got as big as fifty cent pieces. "Ace! What happened?!"

Ace looked at his left shoulder and saw that it was drenched in blood.

"What the fuck?" He reached up and felt the hole

in his head. When he took his hand away it was covered in blood. He stared at his hand dumbfounded, then looked at Amaya and passed out.

Chapter 11

When Los finally regained consciousness, the fluorescent lights in the hospital room set his eyes on fire. He blinked a couple of times until his eyes adjusted, then he looked over to his right and saw Amaya sitting in the chair covered in a blanket watching TV. It might have been the drugs, but to Los it looked like she was glowing. Like she was an angel or something.

He could tell that she was uncomfortable in that chair because she kept moving around. She looked at him then back at the TV. Then she did a double take. Amaya's face lit up as she jumped up from the chair. She ran over to the bed and grabbed Los' hand.

"Hey." She said softly as she ran her hand over his head. "I'm so glad you're awake baby. You just don't know."

"How......" Los cleared his throat." How long I been out?" He asked in a low raspy voice.

"Three weeks. I swear that everything that could possibly have gone wrong has gone wrong."

"What happened?"

"Hold on baby. I'm gonna fill you in. Your dad and Jay wanted me to call them when you woke up." She ran over to her purse and pulled out her phone.

"Where is everybody else?" Amaya ignored him as she called Jay and Alabaster. By the time she got off the phone a couple nurses had come into the room and they did their little check ups on Los. After about fifteen minutes they left and Amaya sat in the bed with him. "Where is Moe?" Amaya looked down at the floor then back up at him.

"Baby, Moe didn't make it." Los closed his eyes and took a deep breath. "Magdalena?"

"She didn't make it either. And you flat lined twice. It's a miracle that you're still here." He didn't respond, he just laid there with his eyes closed and T-Rock's face stuck in his mind.

"I thought you said he was awake." Alabaster said as he entered the room. Los opened his eyes and saw his father and Jay walking through the door. "I know you was my got damn son. Pull through this shit like a true soldier."

"What up my nigga? You aight?" Jay asked as he walked around the bed. "Where is everybody?"

"Shit. This is it." Jay said solemnly.

"What the fuck yo mean, this is it?" Los asked as he struggled to sit up. "Baby you need to lay down."

"Niggas is twisted. Vic and T-Ko got knocked by the Feds. O got murdered in the raid. Ace got shot in the head, now he's in a coma. Moe dead. Maggy dead. Shit is real fucked up right now my nigga. Me and Amaya been keeping shit together out here." Jay explained. Los fell back on the bed as his mind processed what he had just heard.

"Tell him the rest of it." Alabaster said as he took a seat in the chair. "Gone head boy." Jay looked at Los and shook his head.

"T-Rock and his crew hit the house. They got everything, and they burned the fuckin' house down so now we're basically broke and homeless with most of our crew dead, laid up in here or in jail. It's fucked up my nigga."

"What happened to Vic?"

"They got knocked with twenty birds and O went out blazin' like a G."

"O went out like a sucka. You can fight a case lil nigga. You can't fight no got damn bullets." Alabaster said standing up. "I know that shit ugly for you right now, but you can't dwell on this shit. Lick your got damn wounds and come holla at me if you tryna get back on your feet. I don't know where you found this lil thang at, but she's a keeper lil nigga." He said pointing at Amaya. "I'm about to go. Ya'll got my number." Alabaster chunked up the deuces and walked out of the room.

"That's some daddy you got Los." Amaya joked.

"Fuck that nigga. I can't believe this shit."

"Well believe it playa. We aint got shit. I been out here robbin' muthafuckas and lil mama been doin' her thing. I was on some shit when she called me."

"What happened to the Jag?"

"Man. They fucked that car up nigga. Totaled it." Los slowly sat up and slid out of bed. He was so weak that Jay had to help him sit up. "Aye my nigga. I think you need to lay back down."

"I aint finna sit in this muthafucka and not do

nothing. I got business to fuckin' handle."

"Baby he's right. You need to get some rest."

"I been fuckin' restin' for tramp weeks." He snapped.

"Well at least let me go get you some clothes and shit." Jay said as he guided Los over to the chair. "Give me like thirty minutes." Los took a deep breath then nodded.

"Aight. Hurry up."

"I'll be right back." Jay ran out of the room and not even ten seconds later the door opened back up and Denise stuck her head in. She held a hand over her mouth as she walked into the room. The whole time Amaya sat there gritting on her.

"Oh my God. Los you're up." She ran over to him and gently gave him a hug and a kiss on the cheek. "You had me so worried."

"Why the fuck would you be worried?" Amaya asked as she stood up. Denise turned around and looked Amaya up and down.

"Who the fuck are you?"

"That's the exact same thing I was about to ask yo bitch ass."

"Bitch? Hold u one muthafuckin' minute"

"Aye!! Ya'll need to cut that shit out. There aint no fuckin' need for all that. Amaya this is

Denise. Ace's lil sister. Denise, this is Amaya." They both stood there eyeing each other down. "There aint no need for ya'll not to get along and I really don't need the drama. I got too much goin' on as it is."

"So I hear, but I hate to say it, but you aint heard everything yet." Denise said turning her back to Amaya.

"What now? Is it Ace?" Denise looked over her shoulder at Amaya.

"Can you give us some privacy?"

"For what?"

"What is it D?" Los asked impatiently.

"Seriously, I need to talk to you alone. This aint for everybody's ears." Los looked up at Amaya and nodded towards the door.

"Give us a minute mama."

"That's some bullshit nigga." She said pointing at Los.

"Amaya give me a minute." He said with more authority in his voice. Amaya sighed before storming out of the room and slamming the door behind her. "Now what is it?"

"Who was that? Your prostitute? Thought I didn't know, huh?"

"That's irrelevant. What's goin' on? Is it your bro?"

"No. But he still hasn't come out of the coma. They keep saying that he's going to recover, but it's been damn near a month. I know that you have a lot on your plate right now, but I have something important to tell you."

"Spit that shit out then."

"I'm pregnant Los."

"Maaan." Los said as he laughed and rubbed his face. "I thought you was on birth control. Aint that what you told me?"

"The pill is only ninety nine percent effective and we slipped through the cracks with that one percent."

"We? How you even know it's mine?" Denise stepped back, put her hand on her hip and stared at Los surprised.

"I aint no fuckin' hoe nigga. And you was the only person I slept with six weeks ago. I'll give you a DNA test or whatever, but this baby is yours." Los just sat there rubbing his temples. "I just thought you should know." She said before walking out. Los wanted to call after her, but he couldn't bring himself to. There was entirely too much shit going on and he felt like he was going to overload.

About twenty minutes later Jay showed back up with some clothes and Los struggled to get dressed before he snuck out of the hospital. Before leaving he stopped by to see Ace in ICU and saw Denise and their mother. Jay stayed in the hallway with Amaya so she wouldn't feel weird while Los was in the room. Rachel, Ace's mother, stood up and gave Los a hug.

"God was with you boy. He really was." She looked over at her son and a tear fell from her eye. "I pray that the Lord will let me keep my son. He's suppose to bury me. Not the other way around." Los wiped the tear from her cheek.

"Ace gone pull through this. I know he will, but on everything I am Ima get who did this to him."

"No baby." Rachel said shaking her head. "It's a perpetual cycle Carlos. If you don't walk away from it now it'll never stop. You're young, you have a long road ahead of you. Just live your life baby. Leave it alone." Los grabbed her hand and looked her directly in the eyes.

"I'm sorry mama, but I just can't do that. I love ya'll, you hear me." He gave Rachel a hug then looked over at Denise who was sitting in a chair crying. They stared at each other for a few seconds before Los turned around and left the room. He walked straight past Amaya and Jay and headed down the hallway. They looked at each other before speed walking to catch up with him.

"So what's the plan my nigga?" Jay asked.

"I don't know, but T-Rock got it comin'. On my muthafuckin' mama Ima kill that nigga."

Chapter 12

Young Hope

Jay took Los by the house and what he saw made his blood boil. Boards covered the windows and crime scene tape was strung up everywhere. They had been staying at the Northwest Inn in St. Ann, so that's where they took Los. He shacked up for a few days, calling around, smoking weed and popping pain killers.

Three days after he left the hospital Los got in touch with his boy Hollow out in East St. Louis. Hollow was a big monkey ass nigga that Los used to sell work to. He sold dope, but his main hustle was guns. Los could hit him up for anything and Hollow would produce it. He hit the nigga up, told him what the deal was and set up a meeting with him.

At 11:45 pm Los, Jay and Amaya pulled into the Johnny DeShields housing projects. It was almost midnight, but that didn't stop the hood from buzzing with activity. As soon as they pulled up into the parking lot by the rec center Los spotted Hollow. He wasn't hard to pick out of the crowd. He was easily the biggest nigga out there and the big ass chain that hung around his neck glistened under the street lights.

"Pull over there." Los directed from the passenger seat. Jay parked in a vacant parking spot right in front of where Hollow stood with a group of niggas. When he threw the car in park Amaya got out and opened up Los' door.

"Got damn baby. What up?" One of the niggas said as Los got out of the car. Hollow put his hand on the nigga's shoulder.

"Fall back youngin'. That's my patna's chick." He said as he approached the car with a beer bottle in his hand. He shook Los' hand and pulled him into a half hug. "My nigga you look like shit." Hollow said as he stepped back to check him out. "You done lost a lot of weight man."

"I know. That's what happens when you take three bullets nigga."

"Yea, I heard about that shit. I'm glad you pulled through."

"Hell yea. This Amaya and that's my nigga Jay, I was telling you about." Los said as Jay got out of the car. Hollow shook both of their hands then gestured for them to follow him into one of the apartments.

"Come on. Let's go inside." They went into the apartment with Hollow and followed him upstairs to one of the rooms. When they walked in the bed was covered with guns and ammunition. "Check that shit out." He said pointing to the bed. Los and Jay walked over and began to examine the hardware. Hollow went into the closet and came back out with two bullet proof vests. "You might need these." Jay took them from him and handed one to Los.

"I shoulda been had one."

"You slippin'." Hollow said as he took a sip of beer.

"So what you gone hit a nigga for all this?" Los asked.

"That's two chops, two Mossberg pumps. That's sixteen hundred right there. Four nines, two 357's. Twenty six hundred. Four extra clips. Twenty eight. I usually hit niggas five for the vests, but Ima let ya'll get em for three fifty. That's uh, Thirty five and Ima let ya'll win with the ammo. Just give me Thirty six hundred and you walk away with everything on that bed."

"Bet that." Los nodded at Jay and he counted out thirty six hundred dollars as Los and Amaya loaded the guns into the black duffel bags. "Good lookin' out my nigga." Los said as he lifted one of the bags off the bed.

"You know what it is. If you need anything else don't hesitate to call a nigga." "Believe me. I won't." They shook hands again and Los, Amaya and Jay dipped out. They had a whole lot of shit to do.

Chapter 13

Los was slowly regaining his strength, but he was still too weak to be running into gun fights, so he just chilled and looked the situation in. He didn't like that Amaya and Jay were carrying him though, so he finally gave in and called Alabaster. Los was just ready to get it on, so he put up with the twenty minute lecture his father seemed to have prepared for him. Eventually he said, fuck it, and interrupted him.

"Man, you said call you if I was tryna to get back on my feet. Well, I called you nigga. Is you fuckin' wit me or not?"

"I told you I was muthafucka. Ima introduce you to some people, so dress like you got some class and leave that street shit at the door."

"Aight."

"I'll call you in the morning."

"It's on." Los hung up and shot over to the mall to find something to wear. The next morning he was up at the crack of dawn. He hit the shower, got fresh then posted by the phone while he smoked a blunt and watched the news. At eight o'clock on the dot his cell phone went off. He snatched it up off the and table and put iat to his ear. "Yea?"

"Bring yo ass downstairs. I aint got all day." When Los got outside Alabaster and his bodyguard were sitting in the parking lot in the Range Rover. As soon as Los slid into the back seat and closed the door Alabaster turned around and wa on him.

"Now I been doin' business with these cats for a long muthafuckin' time. Don't go in there and embarrass me with all that tough boy shit."

"What the fuck is you talkin' about?" Don't come at me like I'm one of those off brand niggas man. I know how to fuckin' conduct myself." Los shot right back instantly taking offense.

"You heard what I said." Alabaster added before turning back around in his seat. Los blew him off and the rest of the ride was dead silent. They went out to O'Fallon and pulled up in front of a modest brick house with a black Lincoln town car parked in the driveway. When they got out of the truck and walked up on the porch a big well dressed Hispanic man opened the door before they could even knock.

They walked into the nearly empty living room and the bodyguard closed and locked the door. Los just watched as the bodyguard approached Alabaster and his driver. They nonchalantly put their hands up in the air and he began to pat them down. When he was done he looked over at Los and motioned for him to come over.

Los looked at Alabaster then back at the bodyguard before walking over to him and raising his arms. The bodyguard started patting him down and stopped when he got to the small of Los' back. Los lifted up his jacket and produced a fat chrome 357. Los handed the burner to him and he led them through the kitchen and into the basement.

The basement was decked out like a little lounge with a big flat screen, pool table and wet bar. Los instantly spotted two more Hispanic men sitting in front of the TV. When they descended the stairs the two men stood up to greet Alabaster and his bodyguard. One of them was significantly older with a very intense look in his eyes. The other one looked like he was in his later twenties and he had a laid back demeanor.

"So this is the one who's suppose to take Victor's place?" The older man asked as he sized Los up.

"Yea, that's my youngest son, Carlos. Carlos this is Juan and his son Jr." Los nodded then shook both of their hands.

"You look a little young to be entering this line of work." Juan said.

"Don't let the looks fool you Juan. That boy there was born for this shit."

"I like him." Jr interjected as he downed a shot of cognac. Everybody looked at
Jr and Los couldn't help but ask.

"How do you know? I haven't said a single word."

"You don't need to say anything. It's your eyes." Jr said pointing at his temple with his index finger. "They're sharp, alert, hard and you make good eye contact. A man is a man when he can look you in the eyes and not flinch." Jr looked over at Juan. "What do you think?" Juan continued to look Los in as he rubbed his chin.

"I definitely see potential, but he's a kid"

"How old are you Carlos?" Jr asked.

"Eighteen, but........" He held up his hand and cut Los off.

"Do you know what you're getting yourself into?"

"Of course I do." He stated confidently.

"Ok. This is what I'll do since me and your father have history and I like you. Bring me fifteen grand and I'll give you one kilo of ninety percent pure. You won't find anything as pure as mine. Not in these neck of the woods. Now, you do that and we'll go from there."

"Aight. I appreciate you taking a chance on me too. That means a lot."

"I have a feeling about you Carlos. Probably the same feeling my father had about Alabaster." Los looked over at his father and had to admit that even though he was a wack ass dad the nigga was a certified hustler. They sat around in the basement for a little while longer before finally leaving. When they got into the Range Rover Alabaster turned around and smiled.

"You did good boy. You did real good. I can give you the fifteen racks if you need in." He offered. Los just shook his head and looked out the window.

"Naw. I got it."

****

That night Los called and set u a special visit to see his brother. The next morning at ten am Los and Amaya were sitting in the visiting room waiting for Vic to come. When Vic walked into the booth he sat down and picked up the phone with a bland look on his face. Los stared at his big bro for a few seconds before picking up the phone on his side of the glass.

"You aint happy to see me nigga?" Los asked with a little smirk.

"Hell yea! You just don't know. I fuckin' went left when I heard what happened to you lil nigga. I still aint right."

"I can tell. Man you look like shit bro." Vic sighed as he rubbed his temples. He really did look like shit. One look at him and Los could tell that stress was kicking his ass. He had lost weight and his eyes had dark circles around them.

"This shit is ugly in here my nigga. I'm stressed the fuck out."

"What the hell happened? I been hearin' bits and pieces, but I wanna hear it from the horse's mouth."

"I was fuckin' slippin'. I can't really go into no detail, but basically I got pulled over because the tag on the car I was in was expired. I got a ticket and the cop let me park the car at White Castle and call for a ride when two fuckin' cars full of Feds pop up. The booked me, searched the car, found a tool and a trunk full of groceries." He explained as he shook his head.

"How much was it?" Vic set the phone down and flashed Los ten fingers. "Got damn bro." He said as Vic put the phone back up to his ear. "What's up with T-Ko?"

"They raided the spot and ended up killin' O and T-Ko got hit with four thangs and manufacturing a dangerous controlled substance. As far as I know he's still holdin' it down."

"What you lookin' at my nigga?" Vic shrugged his shoulders.

"I got a pretty good lawyer, but we don't even know yet. They aint even offered a nigga nothing. I guess they tryna see who turns first. Me or T-Ko."

"Well, I got some shit in motion. If you need anything just let me know my nigga."

"I will."

"I wish you wasn't behind that glass cuz I actually got something for you."

"Like what?" Los held up his index finger like hold on and looked over at Amaya and said something. She looked around suspiciously before going underneath her long dress and removing a condom full of weed from her stash spot. She handed it to Los and he held it up for Vic to see.

"You ever smoke some white widow?"

"You know I have nigga. I need some smoke too."

"How you gone get it?" Vic looked around then got up and walked over to a nigga who was wearing a white T with the word Trustee stenciled on it. They talked for about a minute before Vic walked back over and got on the phone.

"There should be a ledge on the bottom of our counter. Just put it there and I'll get it."

"How?"

"Come on Los. This is big bro. I make shit happen."

"Yea aight man." Los said as he put the weed in the spot. They visited for another twenty minutes before the CO came in and told them they had to leave. Los said goodbye to his big brother and told him that he'd see him next week. But in the mean time he had to figure out how he was going to come up with fifteen thousand dollars.

Chapter 14

"Man this is some fuckin' bullshit." Los said as he plopped down on the couch of the kitchenette motel room. Jay sat his gun down on the table and ashed his black and mild.

"What we gone do? I done did everything I could think of and aint shit comin' together."

"This don't make no sense. I was just havin' hundreds of thousands now a nigga struggling to come up with a lousy fifteen. It's fuckin' pitiful." Los said as he sat there pouting. It had been three days since he met Juan and Jr and all he had managed to ome up with was sixty five hundred between him and Jay. He could have just hit his pops up for the cash, but he didn't want to give Alabaster the satisfaction.

"We could hit up this dice game later on." Jay suggested.

"I hate robbin' dice games. It be too much activity so that shit be sloppy man." Los said as he started to roll up a blunt.

"I aint say shit about robbin' it nigga."

"Hell naw. We can't gamble with none of that money Jay."

"Well what the fuck we gone do then?" Los stopped rolling the blunt, looked at Jay and was about to respond when they heard somebody fumbling with the lock on the front door. Los and Jay quickly grabbed their burners and walked towards the door with their fingers on the triggers. The door swung open and Amaya stood there scared shitless as she was met with two fat barrels.

"It's me, it's me." She said as she dropped her purse and put her hands up. Los lowered his gun before bending down, snatching up her purse and pulling her inside. He stuck his head out and scanned the hallway before closing the door. "Ya'll are crazy."

"Why the fuck you aint been answerin' your phone Amaya?!" Los questioned as he forcefully handed her back her purse.

"This dumb ass trick spilled beer all over it." She said as she pulled it out of her purse to show him.

"You act like we just got money to blow or something." Amaya just smiled and reached into her bra and produced a wad of one hundred dollar bills.

"I got that from the dumb ass trick. It's five grand." She said proudly. "But that's not even the half of it. I know for a fact that if you ran up on him you could come out with at least twenty thousand. The muthafucka is a complete moron, but he has money out the ass. I figured you could rob him, then you'd have enough to do what you needed to do." Los looked up from the stack at Jay then at Amaya in disbelief.

"You serious?"

"Yea daddy. Why would I play? I know how serious the situation is."

"Well, where the fuck is he?"

"He stays in those apartments behind Holman middle school. I'm supposed to be going back over there later on."

"And this shit is guaranteed?" Los probed as he looked Amaya dead in the eyes.

"Yes. I didn't count it, but from bein' around you I kinda learned how to eyeball stacks and it was at least twenty grand if not more in the nigga's freezer." Los looked at Jay and smiled.

"You game for a 211 ?"

"Pst. What type of fuckin' question is that nigga? My name should be 211, while you bullshittin'."

"Aight." Los looked back at Amaya. "Go hit that water baby girl. We need you tip top for this, you understand me?" She flashed Los that million dollar smile, nodded and he slapped her on that million dollar ass as she strutted towards the bathroom. Los tucked his pistol and motioned for Jay to follow him back into the living room.

****

Tony was a thirty five year old schizophrenic who was obsessed with cartoons and video games. When he took his medication like he was suppose to, he was halfway normal. But still not normal enough to have personal relationships with anybody besides his toy collection. It wasn't that he didn't want to have friends or a girlfriend, but he was a certified weirdo and nobody really wanted to have nothing to do with him.

Then he met Amaya. They were inside the lobby of the Jack In The Box across the street from the middle school. When he first saw her, he was sitting at a table eating and she was standing at the counter looking like an Egytian goddess. When she got her food, she turned around and caught him staring, so she decided to come and sit right next to him. It was obvious to her that he was a weirdo, but in her line of work the weirdos always seemed to pay the best.

"Hey stranger." She flirted as she took her seat.

"Hi." He replied putting his head down and focusing on her food. She sized him up and noticed the bag sitting next to him. Amaya strained her neck to see what was inside and saw that it was an action figure and a couple of video games.

"Do you mind if I check that out?" SHe asked pointing to the bag. He looked up at her surprised.

"This?" He asked as he picked the bag up.

"Yea. Just for a second." Tony reluctantly handed Amaya the bag and she made a show of pulling out the action figure." I thought that was what this was. I've been looking for one of these." She lied.

"Oh, you like Lord of the Rings?"

"Of course. Who doesn't? How much did this thing cost you?"

"I think it was a hundred and seventy five dollars. I don't know. The receipts in the bag." Amaya fished the receipt out and dollar signs popped up in her eyes.

"You spent three hundred and eighty dollars on

video games and one toy?" She asked incredulously.

"Well that 'toy...'" He said using his fingers as quotation marks." It's a collectors item and it'll be worth a lot of money one day."

"I'm just sayin' baby, you spending all of your money on inanimate objects whe you could just buy this toy right here and I promise it'll be the last toy you ever buy." She said seductively.

"What do you mean?" He asked nervously.

"Buy me and find out. You'll never get tired of playing with this."

"How much?" From there it was curtains for poor old Tony. Amaya went with him back to his apartment and put it on him. After three minutes it was over and she had an extra five hundred just to sit and talk. It was almost too easy for her. Amaya pushed her luck to try and see what all she could get out of the weird nigga.

She told him that her car was in the shop and that she needed five thousand to get it out. Tony bit the bait instantly and offered to give her the five grand. Amaya followed him into the kitchen and watched as he went into the freezer and counted out four racks. She thought about cracking him over the head and taking everything, but there was a big size difference between the two of them and if she didn't knock him out off the flop, she wouldn't last long in a fight.

Instead, Amaya just decided to play it safe. She got the money form Tony and told him that she'd come back later on before leaving. That's all Tony could think about all day. He sat around in a daze replaying that three minutes over and over in his head. When he finally heard a knock at the door his heart damn near jumped from his chest. He quickly stood up and literally ran to the door and snatched it open.

There she was, even more beautiful than she was earlier that day. Just looking at her made his stomach do cartwheels. He had never experienced love, but he knew he was in love with her. He just wanted to grab her and tell her how much he loved her, but that fantasy shattered when Los and Jay appeared in the doorway wearing ski masks. Los palmed Tony's face and pushed him down to the floor as they bulldogged their way into the apartment.

"Don't hurt him." Amaya whined as she closed and locked the door.

"Shut up." Los demanded pointing at her with his index finger. He trained his 357 on Tony and nodded towards the kitchen as he looked at Jay. "Go get what we came for." Jay nodded before casually walking into the kitchen.

"What's this about?" Tony asked from the floor.

"It's nothing personal nigga. Just lay there and be quiet. This'll be over in a minute." Los said as they heard Jay in the kitchen tearing shit up. Tony looked up at Amaya through some big puppy dog eyes.

"You set me up. I thought you liked me."

"I do, but business is business sweety."

"But, but I love you." Los lightly kicked him in the ribs.

"Aye man shut the fuck up." He said before looking at Amaya. "Go find something to tie this nigga up with." Five minutes later Tony was hog tied on the floor of his living room and they were leaving with all of the money he had saved up. Before walking out the door Amaya turned around and mouthed the words.

"I'm sorry."

Chapter 15

"I knew that I liked you." Jr said as he pointed at Los with his cigar. "My pop and your pop, they're old school. I'm not a youngster anymore, but I'm young enough to pay attention to what's current. Your brother was current, but you got something different about you. I just can't put my finger on it, but I can tell that we're going to do great business together."

"You can bank on that." Los replied cooly as he sat across from Jr. He had called Jr up earlier that day and agreed to meet him. When Los showed up he dropped thirty thousand dollars in Jr's lap.

"I know I can."

"So, what we lookin' at?" Jr sat there staring at Los as his mind went to work. "Wait right here. I'll be back in a minute." Jr stood up, collected the thirty racks and went upstairs. Fifteen minutes later Jr re-emerged carrying three small bricks. He dropped them on the couch next to Los.

"A gesture of good faith. I believe in you Carlos. Don't let me down."

"Don't worry about it man. Success is my only option." When Los left Jr's pad he went straight to the tele and got in the kitchen. Amaya and Jay were there waiting on him so they already had everything ready for him to whip some shit up. Los soaked a bandana in water and covered up his face with it so he wouldn't get high while he was doing his do.

By the time the sun set they had all three birds rocked up and bagged as individual zips. Luckily for them Northwest Inn was a breeding spot for potential smokers. Amaya had befriended a local prostitute named Sunshine. She was a little older, but Los could tell that back in the day she had been easy on the eyes. Sunshine and her two bit pimp, Taylor, both smoked crack and they kept a lot of traffic in and out of their hotel room.

Los broke them off a quack and set up shop. Amaya did her thing, Los picked up a couple of the clients he had before he got shot, and Jay ran the streets making moves like he always did. In two weeks the three of them sold three bricks basically stone for stone. They came back with almost a hundred and fifty thousand dollars and Los took ninety to Jr and got six more.

The money was flowing in and fast. Extremely fast, but Los and Jay never lost sight of what they still had to do. T-Rock was out there running around living it up while Moe and Magdalena decayed in the ground and Ace sat in the hospital
in a coma. He didn't know it yet, but he had a set date with the devil.

****

T-Rock felt untouchable. Like he was the shit. He had everything he ever wanted. More money than he could count, cars, clothes, females. After the lick his life did a complete 360. Nights on the prowl looking for somebody to rob turned into nights at the spot clocking. As much as T-Rock hated Los he had to admit that the nigga had style, so he went and copped a Jaguar out of spite.

Muthafuckas from the hood would say that he had everything, but T-Rock would disagree vehemently. It was true, he had a lot of material items, but life was still ill. His baby mama was in a wheel chair and probably wouldn't ever walk again. Then he still had to carry a shit bag around on his hip everywhere he went, but what really had him jittery was the fact that Los and Ace were still alive.

He had followed the story on the news and when he found out that Ace survived a bullet to the head he knew shit was going to be ugly. But after surgery Ace went into a coma. Then Los woke up and had been in the streets, but hadn't retaliated yet. It drove T-Rock insane because he knew they were going to come after him, but he didn't know when.

His thoughts were interrupted when Jacco and Cynthia walked into the house laughing and giggling like they had just heard the funniest shit in the world.

"Sup bro. What you in here doin'?" Cynthia asked as she took a seat next to him on the couch. T-Rock just shook his head dismissively."What's wrong with you?"

"Aint shit wrong with me. What the fuck is wrong with you?" He lashed out. "Whoa cuz, cool ya jets. Let me scream at you outside." Jacco cut in. T-Rock stood up with an attitude and followed his cousin out onto the porch. "I know that you stressing about ya baby mama and shit, but you can't be takin' that shit out on ya peoples nigga. We all dealin' with it together. That's what family for cuz."

"First off, you don't know what the fuck goin' on nigga. You aint gotta shit in a got damn bag, so you can miss me with all that shit." T-Rock spat as he got up in Jacco's face.

"You betta pipe down lil nigga."

"Pipe down? Fuck you think this is? The only reason you got anything is cuz of me. Nigga, I mad you. You aint shit!" Jacco pushed T-Rock hard making him stumble back. When T-Rock regained his balance he socked Jacco right in the jaw. A couple punches were exchanged before they grabbed each other and started to tussle. They didn't even notice the little nigga ride up in the yard on a bike.

"T-Rock!! T-Rock, somebody just shot up your spot!" They let each other go and looked at the little nigga.

"What?" He asked incredulously.

"Some dudes came through with some big ass guns and started shooting. I came straight over here." T-Rock ran back into the house and re-emerged with a 12 gauge shotgun in his hands. They took off running up the street and when they got to the spot T-Rock stopped in the front yard and just stared at the house with his blood boiling.

One of his boys, Nate, was the only one who was in the house at the time. He sat on the porch of the bullet riddled house puffing on a cigarette. He couldn't stop his hands from shaking even if he tried.

"What the fuck happened?!" Jacco asked as he approached the house.

"Aint it fuckin' obvious." He replied sarcastically as he gestured to the scene behind him. "I swear to God it seemed like they shot this muthafucka up for twenty minutes."

"Who was it?"

"How the fuck should I know? I was hidin' nigga. Look at that got damn house." T-Rock just shook his head as he looked around the block. A lot of nosey neighbors were standing on their porches and watching safely from their windows. T-Rock ran his free hand over his face as the faint sound of police sirens caught his ears.

"Yo Jacco, we gotta go!" He said as he stuck the long barrel of the shotgun down his pant's leg. As soon as T-Rock turned to walk away his cell phone started going off in his pocket. He didn't slow down as he answered.

"What up?"

"Oh my God Thomas, somebody just shot up the houser!" Cynthia informed him in a frantic voice. In the background he could hear his mother and his baby crying and screaming. He couldn't even respond. He just broke into a sprint and ran home. When he bent the corner his mother was standing in the middle of the street holding his son while Cynthia stood in the driveway on the phone with the police.

T-Rock could tell from way up the street that the house was shot to shit. It was unreal. Like a scene from an action movie or something. He knew what it was and exactly who was responsible. War had been officially declared. Nothing and no one was off limits. It was open season and T-Rock knew that that was the message Los was sending. And the message was heard loud and clear.

Chapter 16

Los was on some shit. Ever since he got out of the hospital, he had been in a real dark place, but after they shot up T-Rock's spot and his mama's house, he was feeling like a new nigga. He held the cards. Nobody that was in the streets like that knew that he was staying in a hotel, so he wasn't even worried about T-Rock retaliating, but staying on point was a habit and he kept a burner in close proximity.

The next morning when Los got up he woke Amaya up and took her to the car dealership with him. An older white man greeted them as soon as they walked through the doors. He couldn't take his eyes off of Amaya as he shook Los' hand.

"Excuse me, I am so sorry for staring, but your beauty is just so breathtaking." He said before looking back at Los who stood there with an interested look on his face. "You are a lucky young man." Los shrugged his shoulders.

"That's one way to look at it."

"Well, what can I help you two with this morning.?" The salesman asked rubbing his hands together. "We have an extensive selection of automobiles. Luxury coupes, sedans, SUV's."

"I'm not sure what I want. You think we can go check out a couple cars?"

"Yes. Yes of course." The salesman led them outside to the lot. "What kind of car did you come here in? Are you trying to upgrade, trade?"

"We came in a cab." Los answered blandly as his eyes scanned the lot. "Oh. Well, do you have any specific tastes?"

"Not really.." Los looked back at Amaya who was quietly walking behind them. He followed her gaze and saw that she was locked in on a silver Benz. "You like that car mama?"

"It's cool, I guess." She said nonchalantly. Los stopped and pointed the car out to the salesman.

"What's up with that one?"

"That's the 2010 Mercedes Benz 5400. Personally one of the best cars I've ever driven."

"Let's check it out." Los put his arm over Amaya's shoulders and started walking towards the car. When they got up on it Los slid into the passenger seat and Amaya got behind the wheel. "This muthafucka clean."

"Everything comes as is. GPS and navigation, the TV screens "

"I hate to cut you off." Los said interrupting him. "But I need to holla at my girl real quick."

"Oh, of course. Just let me know when you find something you're interested in."

"Aight, I will." Los said dismissively and the salesman headed back into the building.

"You gonna get this car?" Amaya asked as she ran her hands ever the wood grain steering wheel.

"Should I?"

"I can't say if you should or not. I mean, I think that you deserve it and it is a nice car."

"Would you drive it?"

"Hell yea, I would. It's a Benz." She said matter of factly.

"You want it?" She looked at Los with a mixture of shock and disbelief on her face.

"No, I couldn't.. ..... " Amaya said shaking her head.

"Of course, you can. You just said that I deserve this car and I do, but you do too. You been pullin' your fuckin' weight and I don't say how much I appreciate you enough. I never told Magdalena that shit and now it's too late. But you been there with a nigga since day one and you been goin' hard for a nigga. I just wanna show you that you dear to me Amaya."

"Oh Los." She said softly as her eyes started to tear up.

"Don't start that shit man." Amaya leaned across the middle console and hugged him.

"Thank you so much."

"Naw. Thank you." When Amaya got composed they went back into the building and found the salesman sitting at his desk in his office. "Yo. Ima need two of them. The one off the lot and a black one."

"You want two Benz's?" He asked surprised.

"Yea. That's what I said aint it?"

"Well, I'll have to do a credit check and..."

"Aint no need for all that." Los said as he unzipped his back pack and dropped it on his desk. The salesman's eyes got big as hell when he caught a glimpse of the stacks of money in the bag. "We good?"

"Give me a little while to get the paperwork together and you'll be able to take those babies home today."

"Good man." Los and Amaya sat around in the lobby chopping it up and kicking the shit while the salesman did his job. About an hour and a half later they signed the titles and the leasing contracts and smashed out. Amaya followed him downtown and Los took her to an empty loft that had a nice view of the St. Louis Arch.

"What's this?" She asked as she looked around the spacious loft. "This is where muthafuckas gone live."

"There's no walls."

"No shit. It's a loft. It aint gone cost that much to throw up some drywall though. You like it?" She shrugged as she continued to look around.

"It's big." Was all she said The loft was barren. She could tell that it hadn't been lived in in a long time, if ever. There was no carpet anywhere, the floors were plain cement and the walls were bare red brick. "What made you pick this place?"

"A couple reasons. First dude sold it to a nigga for

ten grand and I couldn't pass that up. Then look at this place. All this potential, that view and this muthafucka is off by itself. The seclusion is really what drew me here. Plus we way up on the eighth floor, so can't nobody come shoot this muthafucka up." He said with a little smirk.

"Jay gone stay here too?"

"Naw, this my shit. The homie movin' into a house out there in St. Ann. This muthafucka gone be ready in like a month or two." Los pulled her into a hug and kissed her on the forehead before leaning back and looking her in the eyes. "All that bullshit is behind us Maya. This the beginning of a new chapter you hear me?"

Amaya just gave him a wry smile and nodded her head. As much as she wanted to believe that shit was going to get better the bulletproof vest under Los' hoody told her otherwise. It seemed like they were on their way to improving the current situation, but Amaya knew all too well that shit got worse before it got better.

Chapter 17

Los went into over drive on the grind trip. He had to make back the money he spent on the cars and that loft. Then the renovations were tapping his pockets, but he wasn't tripping, he'd drop whatever for that shit because he was ready to get the fuck out of that hotel. On top of that he was steady kicking Vic and T-Ko down with doe because like jack asses they left their money with bitches and they ran off with that shit.

The situation just made him grind harder. He had people that depended on him so stressing and half stepping weren't available options. One day he stopped by the hospital to see Ace and was surprised when he didn't see Denise or their mother there. The sight of his nigga laying there hooked up to umpteen machines brought tears to his eyes, and he hadn't cried since his mother died.

Los sat beside Ace's bed thinking about how his life had turned around. Shit was happy go lucky and easy when he first went to live with his big brother, but all that changed. He was eighteen years old with three bullet wounds on his body and he sat in a hospital wearing a Teflon vest with a 357 on his hip. But the thing that probable bothered Los the most was that he wouldn't change a single thing.

Except for the Denise situation. There was a strong possibility that he was the father of her unborn child. The father of his best friend's niece or nephew and he was neglecting his responsibilities as a real nigga. Los sat there thinking about if for another twenty minutes before leaving the hospital, hopping in the Benz and heading over to her house. When he got there he walked up to the door and just as he was about to knock the door came open.

Denise was surprised at first, but the look of surprise

on her pretty face quickly turned into one of disdain. She had her purse on her shoulder and sunglasses on her head, so it was obvious that she was headed somewhere. Los couldn't do shit, but stand there and stare. Her stomach wasn't big, but it was obvious that she was pregnant.

"What are you doin' here Carlos?"She asked with an attitude.

"You look good D."

"That doesn't answer my question."

"Do you mind if I come in?"

"I'm on my way to the hospital."

"I just left the hospital. That's why I really need to talk to you. Just give me a few minutes, then I'll leave." Denise let out a sigh before stepping out of the way and letting Los inside.

"You got five minutes." She said as she closed the door. She crossed her arms across her chest and stood there staring at him like a typical pissed off black woman.

"Aight Denise, I know I been on some bullshit." She nodded her head in agreement. "I apologize, cuz that aint the way my mama raised me. It's just been a whole lot goin' on and I aint been myself lately. I'm tryna get my shit together and before I do I gota make things right between us. I know Ace would be ready to kick my ass if he knew what's been goin' on."

"What are you doing? What is this?"

"This is me tryna be in my kid's life. I want to be there for ya'll."

"Los I need a man, not a boy. You aint gone deny my baby and then waltz in here with that elementary ass game and think everything gone be everything."

"Now you on some bullshit." He said pointing at her.

"I aint come over here to argue with you. I came to apologize and let you know that I was ready to accept my responsibilities as a muthafuckin' man. I know you mad at a nigga and you got the right to be, but you aint gotta fuckin' like me for me to take care of my muthafuckin' child."

"Get the hell outta my mama house!" She yelled pointing towards the door.

"Aight." He said shrugging his shoulders as he crossed the living room. "You needa grow up man, but you sittin' up in here actin' like a fuckin' kid." Los said sarcastically. "Ima love you regardless D. You kickin' me out ya mama house won't change that, so when you decide to grow the fuck up, call me." He said as he walked out the door. As Los got into his car his phone went off. He quickly pulled it out of his pocket thinking it was Denise, but it was Hollow trying to cop a nine piece.

Los smashed back to the hotel riding in silence seething about what had just happened. When he got to the hotel he hurried up and pulled out his tools to weigh out Hollow's order. As he scooped the 252 grams of soft into a zip lock bag, Amaya strolled in with a big smile and her keys hanging form her manicured fingers.

"Hey Daddy." She greeted as she walked into the

small kitchen. Los just nodded as he texted Hollow with the blunt hanging from his lip. "You ok?"

"Any reason why I wouldn't be?"

"I don't know." She replied timidly. "You just look like something's bothering you." Los sat his phone down on the counter and began to put everything up. "Well, maybe this will cheer you up." She said handing him a fat wad of money. "Remember the guy who sold you the cars?"

"You got this from him?" He asked as he took the money from her.

"And we didn't even do nothing. Well, I didn't do nothing." She said with a childish grin. Los couldn't help but smile back. Amaya was really something else. A certified gold mine. "I knew I could get a smile outta you."

"You just never cease to amaze me. I don't even know how I came up with you." "I don't either lil daddy." She joked as Jay walked into the room.

"Where you been nigga?" Los asked as Jay closed the door behind him.

"Shit, I been runnin' around, then I stopped by the hospital to see Ace."

"I went by there earlier."

"Oh, so you know." Jay said posting up on the counter.

"Know what?"

"Denise pregnant. Somebody done knocked her up." Los didn't respond and he didn't have to. His face said it all.

"Maaaan. Get the fuck outta here nigga. You got Ace lil sister pregnant?" Jay asked with a wide smile. Amaya turned and looked at Los expecting him to say something.

"So, that's what she wanted to talk to you about that day at the hospital. Why you aint tell me Carlos?"

"Cuz it aint none of your business."

"Like hell it aint! Nigga, I slave for you every fuckin' day. I know that you aint dedicated to me like I am to you, but the least you coulda did was told me." She said getting emotional. Jay just stood there scratching his head with a look on his face like he wish he would have kept his mouth shut. "Then you gone say it aint none of my business like I'm a bitch off the street or something. Thanks for letting me know how you really fuckin' feel nigga." She spat before turning her back to him.

"Amaya......" He grabbed her arm, but she shook loose.

"Get the fuck off me!" She yelled as she headed for the door.

"Man, where the fuck are you goin'?" Amaya ignored his question as she left and slammed the door behind her. Los looked over at Jay like "what the fuck."

"Man, bro just let her cool down. We both know that she aint goin' nowhere." It sounded good, but he just didn't know how wrong he was.

Chapter 18

Young Hope

Los could tell that Amaya was hurt, so he decided to give her some time to calm down. But she didn't pop back up that night. Then the days went by and the days turned into weeks. At first Los was kind of worried about her, but after that second week went by he shrugged her off. He missed having her around and everything, but he had too much shit going on in his life for him to be wasting his time thinking about her.

Los just did his thing in the streets and focused on finishing up his loft. He was so caught up in the streets that he didn't even realize that his birthday had crept up on him, but Jay did. When Jay pointed it out Los shrugged it off and posted up in the spot, but Jay wasn't going for that shit. After a couple blunts and a whole lot of persuasion Jay finally go him to go out to the club.

They got fresh then hopped in the Mercedes and headed out. When they got to the club the parking lot had a life of its own. Los parked and navigated through the crowd of drunk and high people who occupied the lot ot get to the entrance of the club. Two big niggas wearing security shirts stood at the door. When they went to frisk him and Jay, Los protested and pulled out a fat knot.

After peeling both of them off a couple hundred dollars a piece, Los and Jay stepped into the dub clean as a whistle with their pistols on their hips. The dance floor was packed with muthafuckas dancing to "Money To Blow" by Drake/ Lil' Wayne and Birdman. Los went over to the bar and slammed a hundred dollar bill on the counter.

"Aye bartender, let me get a bottle of Patron."

"Make that two." Jay added as he placed another big face on top of Los. The bartender quickly snatched the money up before grabbing two bottles of Patron from the shelf. Los instantly popped the top on his bottle and took a swig. "Now look at all this pussy in here nigga. And you was tryna stay couped up in that fuckin' hotel room. "Jay said as he opened his bottle.

"Fuck the club cuz, I rather count a million bucks." Los replied quoting Jeezy.

"I can dig it, but it's your birthday my nigga. You been doin' ya thing, now it's time to live a little. You're nineteen years old. Act like it." He said as a group of girls walked past eyeing them. Jay reached out and grabbed one of their arms. "Say baby let me holla at you." She looked him in checking out his phat chain and glistening grill before smiling and seductively pushing up on him.

"Buy me a drank."

"Open your mouth and tilt your head back."

"What?" She asked as Jay went into his pocket. When he pulled his hand out he had a little bag with a couple x-pills in it. He removed one from the bag and showed her.

"Open your mouth." She smiled before tilting her head back and opening her mouth. Jay dropped the pill on her tongue and washed it down with a little Patron. "What's your name?"

"Simone and these are my home girls, Debbie, Alexis, Tisha and Vera."

"Well, I'm Jay and this my nigga Los." He said lightly hitting Los in the chest with the back of his hand.

"Today is my nigga birthday ya hear me."

"How old you turnin' baby boy?" Alexis asked.

"Nineteen." Los replied coolly as he sipped his drink.

"Boy you really is a baby." Vera said as she sized Los up.

"I'm tryna show my nigga a good time, but there's only so much I can do know what I'm sayin'."

"You wanna dance birthday boy?" Alexis asked as she grabbed his hand. "Shit, come on." Los nodded at Jay as Alexis led him out on the dance floor. Independent by Webbie started blaring through the speakers and she turned around and looked at Los with a big ass smile.

"Ooh this my song!" She exclaimed as she started rubbing her ass up against his groin. When she felt the pistol on his hip she looked over her shoulder at him and he just shrugged as he hit his bottle. Eventually he relocated the burner to his left back pocket. They danced together through a couple more songs before heading back over to the bar.

Los didn't even make it because a whole 'nother group of bitches swarmed him and Alexis got lost in the crowd. When How Low by Ludacris came on all the bitches on the dance floor went into a frenzy. The group of girls that surrounded Los all started shakin' their asses and he couldn't do shit, but stand there and watch. He felt like a fat kid in a candy store.

A lot of the niggas and some of the females stopped dancing and formed a circle around them. One of the girls, a thick yellow bone, was really enjoying all of the attention, so she looked back at Los and pulled up her skirt exposing her bare ass. Los gave her a heavy handed slap on it as she began to put on a show.

The crowd started to cheer and yell as a couple of the other girls followed suit. The yellow bone bent all the way over and touched her toes giving Los a picture perfect shot. Jay busted through the crowd with Simone and her home girls and when he saw Los his face lit up like a Christmas tree.

"Hell yea nigga!! That's what the fuck I'm talkin' about!" He yelled getting extra hyped. Los pointed Jay out nodding his head to the beat as he poured what was left in his bottle all over the yellow bone's ass. Jay ran over to his nigga and pulled him into a half hug. "I fuckin' love you my nigga! I love you man!"

"You jiggin' nigga. Cut that shit out." Los said, laughing. They maneuvered through the crowd and went back to the bar where Los bought another bottle of Patron.

"You was out there clowin' Los. We need to get them bitches back to the tele man, I promise." Jay said gritting his teeth. Los just shook his head as he popped his second bottle.

"We aint even been here an hour yet. I'm tryna see what I can see." Los took a sip of Patron.

"OI girl comin' over here nigga." Los looked up and saw the yellow bone walking up on him in what seemed like slow motion. She walked right up to him, grabbed his bottle, took a swig then started passionately kissing him. She grabbed his erection through his jeans and whispered something in his ear that made him raise his eyebrows. Los put his arm over her shoulders and chunked up the deuces to Jay.

"I'm finna go to the car real quick." He said with a goofy ass grin.

"It's on bro." As Los and the yellow bone headed for the exit they ran into Alexis, and the yellow bone stuck her tongue out at her. When they got to the car Los lit up the half a blunt that was in the ashtray and the yellow bone went right to work undoing his pants. Los reclined the seat and she buried her face in his lap. He laid there in the seat smoking while she gave him some to the meanest head he had ever gotten. It got to the point where he couldn't take it anymore, so he had to push her off.

"What's wrong?" She asked as she sat up wiping her mouth.

"Not a muthafuckin' thing. I'm just tryna see what that pussy feelin' like."

"Scoot that seat back some more." She said pulling her skirt up. When Los had the seat all the way back she climbed over into his lap facing the windshield. Los went into the middle console and pulled out a condom. Once he had it on she raised up then slowly slid down on it as she held onto the steering wheel. She laid back against his chest as she gyrated and bucked her hips. Los reached in between her thighs and started to massage her clit as he kissed the nape of her neck.

"Keep doin' that." She said softly as she leaned forward and began to bounce her ass in his lap. At first Los continued to play with her pussy, but when she started really putting it on him, he couldn't keep his concentration. "Uhhhh! You enjoyin' this?" She asked as she rocked her hips. "This pussy good aint it?"

"Yea, yo pussy good." Los said biting his lip as she started contracting her muscles on him. He was trying his hardest to stay composed because she had him ready to unload and he hadn't even been in it five minutes yet. "Got damn girl." Los laid his head back and closed his eyes. The sounds of flesh slapping up against flesh and her soft moans sent Los over the edge. He exploded inside the condom just as somebody knocked on the window.

"Ahh fuck!l Yes baby yes!" The yellow bone screamed out as she reached her climax. She went limp up against the steering wheel and Los looked up to see Jay standing by the door. Los opened the door up breathing hard and 'ol girl looked at Jay smiling.

"What up my nigga?"

"I hate to interrupt your lil session." Los held up a hand.

"You straight."

"Well then, get out the car and come check this shit out." Los slapped the yellow bone on the ass and she reluctantly got out of the car pulling her skirt back down. Los pulled the condom off and pulled his pants up before sliding out of the driver seat to see what Jay was talking about. He instantly saw everybody in the parking lot looking towards two groups of niggas.

"Don't even worry about it pimp, Ima kill you. Before the muthafuckin' sum come up nigga you gone be deader then shit." One of the niggas said to somebody from the other group.

"Sound good bitch ass nigga. You wouldn't nust a fuckin' grape in a food fight faggot!" Another nigga shot back.

"Aight. On my mama, Ima kill you nigga. I'll be back." Los turned to Jay.

"Man, what the fuck is this?"

"No. It's fuckin' stupid." Jay grabbed Los' head and made him look at three niggas who were posted up by a burgundy Surburban.

"Aight now look at that." Los' facial expression instantly changed when he saw T-Rock, Jacco and some other nigga. "Say the word and they got. Bottom line." Los looked at Jay just as they heard gun fire break out. They both went for their burners and ducked down behind the Benz until it stopped. When Los glanced up he saw a couple of niggas who were arguing just seconds earlier stretched out on the pavement. Then he looked over at the 'Burban and saw T-Rock and his boys piling into their truck, as the parking lot erupted in chaos.

"Come on! They leavin'." He said as he jumped into the Benz. Jay got into the back seat and the yellow bone tried to get in with him.

"Where the fuck you gain'?" Jay asked.

"With ya'll."

"No the fuck you aint." He said pushing her out

of the car as Los backed out of the parking spot. Los maneuvered through the chaotic parking lot and quickly caught up with the Surburban. He followed T-Rock to a gas station a few blocks away from the club. T-Rock did exactly what Los needed him to do. He parked in the dark on the side of the gas station and Los drove around back.

Nothing needed to be said because Los and Jay were on the exact same page. Los through the car in park and they both hopped out with their guns in hand. They bent the corner and casually walked up on the Surburban as Jacco was getting out of the passenger side. Jacco looked up just as Los and Jay raised their cannons and pulled the triggers.

Five bullets tore into Jacco's body sending him to the ground like a bag of rocks. It was obvious that the nigga in the back seat was reaching for something, so Jay unloaded his clip through the window splattering the nigga's brains all over the inside of the truck. T-Rock just sat there behind the wheel scared shitless.

Los took aim and squeezed the trigger. The first bullet struck T-Rock in his right shoulder and the second shattered the driver side window. Los continued to pull the trigger as he approached the truck, but his gun had jammed up after the second slug left his chamber. He went to open the passenger side door, but Jay grabbed his shoulder.

"Another day, another time bro. Here come them boys." Los snapped back to reality and heard the police sirens. He stole one last glance at T-Rock through the window and wanted nothing more than to literally beat him to death, but that would have to wait until another time. They turned around and ran back to the car and

Young Hope

hopped in traffic.

Chapter 19

The next morning at the crack of dawn, Los woke up with a weird feeling. They had already disposed of the guns in the Mississippi river so he wasn't worried about that, but he just had a gut feeling like something fucked up was going to happen. Los got Jay up and they cleaned the hotel room up until it was spotless. Los took everything that would possibly get him a prison sentence to his semi-furnished loft and on his way back to the hotel he stopped at Steak and Shake.

When Los walked out of the diner he saw two squad cars parked in front of the Inn, but he still got in his car and drove across the street. Never for a second did he think that they were there for him. Los went into the building and when he bent the corner two officers had Jay handcuffed in the hallway. One of the laws looked up and saw Los standing there.

"Hey you! Come here!" He ordered putting his hand on his holstered gun. Los quickly turned around and began to speed walk towards the exit. "Hey stop!" He yelled as he started to pursue him. Los dropped his bags and broke into a sprint. When he got to the door and opened it, he ran right into a black man wearing a cheap suit and even cheaper sunglasses. He grabbed Los and seconds later he was being tackled to the ground from behind. Twenty minutes later Los and Jay were in separate holding cells in the county.

Los sat in the cold small cell for another thirty minutes or so before a CO came in and handcuffed him again. He led Los into a little room with two chairs and a table in it. On the table sat an old out dated tape recorder and up in the corner was a black bubble that contained a video camera. Los took a seat in one of the chairs and waited for a few minutes before the black man in the cheap suit from the hotel walked in carrying a file folder.

"How are you doing Carlos?" He asked as he took off his jacket and set the folder down on the table. Los just sat there looking at the Uncle Tom ass nigga. "I'm detective Keith Winburn with the homicide unit."

"And this is the part where you tell me why the fuck I'm here, right?" Keith pulled a piece of paper from the folder and slid it in front of Los.

"You know why you're here, but before we talk you need to sign this."

"What the fuck is this?"

"You're Miranda rights."

"I aint signin' shit and I don't need to fuckin' talk to you about nothin'. You can take me back to my cell."

"Ok tough shit. I didn't pick you and your friend's names out of a hat. I have a witness that links you to two homicides and an attempted murder, so you can play tough all you want."

"Bullshit! I aint kill no fuckin' body." Los spat convincingly.

"We'll let the lawyers debate that in court."

"You got damn right. Let me make my phone call. I know my muthafuckin' rights." Keith laughed.

"Fuck your rights."

"Fuck you bitch nigga!" Keith went to the door and told the CO to take Los back to the holding cell. When Los got back to the cell he paced the small space with his blood boiling. Witness? The only witness was T-Rock and even though Los thought of T-Rock as a bitch, he didn't take him for a snitch. But then again, snitches weren't snitches until they start snitching.

Los lashed out and punched the solid brick wall like a dumb ass. Nearly breaking his hand. He grunted out in pain as he retracted his arm and cradled his already swelling hand. As he rubbed his fist a familiar voice from the hallway drew him to the small window on the door. Who he saw standing there wearing a blue jump suit with the word "trustee" stenciled on it completely caught him off guard.

"Amaya!" She quickly turned around cutting her conversation short with the other inmate. Amaya dropped her broom and ran over to Los' door when she saw him in the window.

"Oh my God, what are you doing in here?"

"What am I doin? What the fuck are you doin' in here?"

"I had an outstanding warrant for that old possessioncharge."

"How long you been in here?"

"I got pulled over right after I left the hotel that day."

"Man, why you aint call me Maya? I woulda been got

you up outta here. This whole time I thought you had went to Florida or some shit."

"I been trying to get in touch with you, but you're cell phone doesn't accept collect calls. What could I do?"

"As soon as I bond out Ima get you outta here, aight?"

"What did you do?"

"They tryna put two bodies on a nigga."

"Oh Los ....."

"It's a frivolous case mama. I'm finna beat this shit, don't worry."

"I sure hope so."

"Aye, is there a phone out there?"

"Yea. Who do you want me to call?"

"My pops." Los gave her the number and she went and made the call for him. Alabaster said that he'd get Los out, but he still had to sit in that bitch for two days. On the second day Los and Jay went to court and were formally charged with two counts of murder one and one count of attempted murder and the lawyer that Alabaster retained got their bonds set at two hundred and fifty thousand.

Alabaster dropped the fifty thousand required to bond both of them out and later on that day Los and Jay walked out of the county free men. Alabaster griped them out and bitched about the money their little incident had cost him. After that episode was over with Los sat down with the lawyer and he agreed to take Amaya's case.

When Los and Jay got their paperwork it was in black and white who the snitch was. Thomas Arnold bka T-Rock. They had the statement he gave the police that night he got shot where he gave it to them play by play. From how it started back in high school to how it escalated in the streets. The nigga was a certified snitch, but he wouldn't get a chance to say anything on a witness stand. Not if Los had anything to do with it.

Los shot to his loft to reimburse Alabaster, get some money for Amaya's bond and to get her impounded car out. He hit Alabaster off with twenty five racks and then hit the shower. Once he was out and fresh he lit up a fat ass blunt and waited on the lawyer to get at him about Amaya. A few hours later his phone finally rung.

"What up?"

"Hello. Mr. Simms?"

"Yea."
"This is William Archebald."

"Oh yea, what's the verdict?"

"Well, your friend Amaya Hardaway was not granted a bond. The judge seems to think that she's a flight risk."

"Man, you aint even tryin'. How can you get me and the homie a bond on a murder case, but you can't get mama a bond on a lil possession charge?"

"The judge she has is a real hard ass about people that jump bond and supposedly she bonded out before on that same case and went on the run, so he won't give her a bond, but what I did do was talk to the DA. We went to school together and I think I can get her a deal."

"What kind of deal?"

"Two years. She'll end up having to do a minimum of nine months."

"But she aint never been in trouble. What's up with some probation or somethin'?"

"I'll tell you right now that because of the judge she has, probation is out of the question. I'll see what I can do, but that two might be her best bet."

"Aight man." Los said reluctantly. "Just keep in mind that if you work this shit out correctly you might've found yourself a loyal client."

"I will Mr. Simms." When they got off the phone Los called around and located Amaya's Benz. He took a cab to the impound lot and went through hell and back just to get the car back. On his way back to the loft Los stopped by the post office to send Amaya, Vic and T-Ko some money orders. Then he went and whipped up a nine piece so he could provide the streets with that A1 and make some of his money back.

Chapter 20

Los and Jay hit the ground running. First they had to replace the money they lost by catching that case, but more importantly they had to find T-Rock, so he couldn't testify. They looked in every crack and turned over every rock, but that nigga was nowhere to be found, so they rode through and shot his mama's house up again on some hot shit.

The next night they swung through for round two, but T-Rock's mama and sister had moved that quick. So Jay came up with the bright idea to go and shoot T-Rock's baby mama's mama's house. They shot that woman's house to shit and then got out of dodge. Jay went to go fuck with some bitches and Los decided to go to the hospital. When Los walked into the room Ace was still out for the count and Denise was huddled up underneath a blanket in one of the chairs watching TV.

"What up D?" He asked as he walked over and sat in the chair next to hers.

"Hey." She said softly as she sat up in the chair. "You doing ok? I heard about what about what happened with ya'll and T-Rock."

"Yea that shit aint nothin'. How you doin' though? You know with the baby and everything."

"I just had a checkup today and everything seems to be alright. I have an appointment for an ultrasound next week, so I'll finally find out what I'm carryin'."

"That's what's up. What you want it to be?"

"I don't know. What do you want it to be?" She inquired looking Los in the eyes.

"A girl. They say your kids give you ten times the

problems you gave your parents, so I know a lil boy would send a nigga to an early grave."

"You want to come to the appointment with me? I would really like it if you were there."

"Yea. Yea I'll go with you. I wouldn't miss it for nothin' in the world."

"I still can't believe that we're about to have a baby. I just thought that I'd be done with school before I had any kids....."

"You sound like you regret your blessin'."

"That aint it. This just isn't the way I pictured it. I always thought that my baby daddy would be my husband or somethin'."

"Look D, you know a nigga always had feelings for you, but I avoided fuckin' wit you cuz I can't do your right. I'm a fucked up nigga with a fucked up life and I done did some fucked up shit. You deserve better than me."

"That sounds like some self-righteous bullshit to me Los. I know that you're a good person and I know that you would do me right and I know that I deserve better than you, but I'm prepared to lower my standards." She joked getting a little laugh out of him.

"You want a nigga that bad, huh?"

"Boy get over yourself. All I'm sayin' is I love you and you told me that the feeling was mutual, so why aren't we together?"

"I don't know. Maybe because Ima street nigga and I have women that prostitute themselves for me. I don't think I'm prepared to give up my lifestyle to keep it a hunnet."

"I never asked you to. I know who you are Los and I love you just how you are. I wouldn't ever ask you to change a thing I just want you and me to become us. That's all." She said shrugging and looking away. Los stood up and walked over to her. He reached underneath the blanket, grabbed her hand and got her up out of the chair.

"You sure that's what you want?" He asked with his eyes locked on hers.

"I'm positive." She replied as she held his gaze. Los grabbed her waist, pulled her close and pressed his lips up against hers. They stood there exploring each other's mouths with their tongues for a few seconds before Los pulled back and looked at her.

"Now, remember that you asked for this."

"I know what I'm getting into. I think."

"Aight Denise, you sayin' that shit now."

"Boy ..... " She started to say something when she looked over at the bed and saw Ace staring right at them. "Oh my God! Ace!" Los quickly turned around and saw that his boy had finally awaken from his coma. Denise ran over to him and took his hand into hers. "Ace, say something."

"Wha ..... What the fuck are ya'll doin'?" Los busted up laughing as he casually walked over to the bed. "Where am I?"

"You're in the hospital my nigga. You got shot in the fuckin' head and been in a coma for some months." Ace just stared at Los as images started flashing in front of his eyes. He remembered chasing T-Rock down, then blood, a whole lot of blood. Moe's dead body. Magdalena's dead body. More blood. Amaya sitting on the floor with Los' head in her lap. Blood on his fingertips. Nothing. "Yea man you survived a bullet to the head and I can't wait to fill you in on what you been missin'."

Chapter 21

Young Hope

Ace was held in the hospital for a few more weeks for observation, but he still had a long hard road ahead of him. Being incapacitated for so long had a negative effect on his limbs, so when Ace was finally released he had to leave in a wheel chair. Los and Jay both chipped in to pay for Ace's physical rehabilitation therapy because his mother's insurance wouldn't cover it. They weren't tripping, they were just happy to have their homie back.

It didn't take very long for Ace to regain his strength and use of his legs, but he couldn't stay on them for very long, so most of the time when he left the house he had to have his wheel chair. Ace had always been a big cock strong muthafucka, so his situation had him feeling helpless and in a way that shit showed. He wasn't the same nigga he was before he got shot. He was real quiet and gave off a real dark vibe, but he was adamant in voicing his opinion about Los getting his little sister pregnant.

Among a long list of things that was something that had Ace pissed off. Los tried to break everything down to him, but he wasn't hearing it. He didn't approve and wouldn't approve of it, but that shit wasn't what really got to him. All the other bad news he had received when he finally woke up had him twisted. It was like during those few months he was in a coma the whole world had changed.

Los was tired of the way Ace was acting, but he dealt with it because they were boys. All the pouting and depressing shit just pissed Los off because Ace really didn't have anything to be depressed about. Somehow he had walked away from a shot to the head then on top of that he had family and friends that were there for him every step of the way. Los just backed up off of him for a minute to let him get his mind right. Hell, Los had enough shit on his plate.

But one day everybody was busy and Ace didn't have a way to get to his therapy session, so Denise volunteered Los' services. Los didn't mind, so he picked Ace up and took him to his appointment. Neither one of them said anything to each other the whole time. Los dropped him off, went and handled some business then came back when the session was over.

"Where you want me to take you?" Los asked as Ace got into the car.

"My mama's house." He answered with a little mug on his face. Los looked at him, shook his head and turned his music up before pulling out of the parking lot. They rode for a few blocks listening to Urban Legend and Los hit mute on the CD deck.

"Aight my nigga, you's a fuckin' weirdo." He said shooting Ace a sideways glance.

"Fuck you talkin' about?"

"Nigga you be mopin' around sulkin' and shit like you got the fuckin' weight of the world on your shoulders. Aight nigga, you got shot. Boo fuckin' hoo. You still here aint you? I don't know what your deal is, but you need to get over that shit. Straight up. I don't deal with sensitive ass niggas."

"Who you callin' sensitive?"

"You nigga." He spat matter of factly. "Everybody goin' through somethin'. That's a given, but the problems a nigga gotta deal with really don't matter. The only thing that matters is how you deal with them fuckin' problems and whatever your problems is, you dealin' with em on some sensitive shit. Sittin' around cryin' and shit like a lil bitch."

"Aye nigga you better watch your muthafuckin' mouth!"

"Pst. Nigga fuck you. I aint gone bite my tongue cuz you know this is some shit you need to hear. I been waitin' for you to come outta that fuckin' coma, so we could do it up like niggas supposed to and when you finally wake up you aint the same nigga. You fuckin' sensitive. The Ace I knew woulda got out of the hospital on some beast shit. I don't know where the fuck you came from, but you need to get your ass on and let me get my muthafuckin' homeboy back. Straight up." Ace just sat there staring out the window pissed off, but he couldn't say shit because he knew Los was telling the truth.

"And I don't know why you in your feelings about me fuckin' with Denise. You outta anybody should know that she's in good hands."

"Why Denise though? You knew she was in school and shit and you went and got her pregnant."

"Man, that shit just happened. You act like I was tryna trap her or somethin' nigga. You know better than that. But on some real shit we shouldn't even have to talk about this. It aint like I'm tryna put her out there."

"You got damn straight. You my guy, but I'd fuckin' kill you." Ace said looking directly at Los.

"I wouldn't expect nothin' less and I got too much

love for you and your moms to even disrespect lil mama like that, so this conversation is really irrelevant." Los said returning Ace's stare. He looked at the dashboard and saw that he was low on gas, so they made a quick detour and stopped at a gas station. "You want somethin' outta here my nigga?" Los asked as he parked at a gas pump.

"Yea man, get me a Gatorade."

"That's it?"

"Yea." Ace said as he opened the door and slowly got out of the car.

"What the hell you think you doin'?"

"Ima pump the gas. I gotta get all the exercise I can, so go do what you gotta do. I got this."

"Aight man." Los went into the store, bought Ace his drink, a pack of Newports and put thirty bucks on his pump. As he was walking out of the store he peeped two older niggas talking by an Escalade on some big rims. Both of the niggas looked up and locked eyes with him as he pulled a cigarette from the pack. Los had a Sig 16 shot nine mil on his waist and he was watching the two niggas intently because from his time in the streets he had turned out to be a regular quick draw McGraw.

Ace looked up from the gas pump and peeped the situation. He instantly went on alert mode, but there really wasn't shit he could do because he didn't have a gun. One of the niggas nodded at Los and to his surprise started to walk towards him. Los never took his eyes off of him as he approached. He was waiting for any wrong moves, so he could go for his gun and lay the stranger down, but as soon as dude got within arm's reach he put his hands up and smiled.

"I aint here to cause no problems lil daddy. You is Los, aint you?"

"Who the fuck are you?" Los asked as he lit his cigarette.

"You don't know me, but I know all about you. I'm Gino, T-Rock's big cousin." Los instantly tensed up debating whether or not to just take off on him. "I know your brother and shit. We used to….."

"I don't give a fuck. What you on nigga? You know I'm into it with T-Rock, so what, you want some too?" Gino smirked as he eyed the young goon.

"I know the whole situation pimp. Ya'll niggas supposed to be the ones who killed my other lil cousin Jacko, but that shit is for another time and place. I'm approachin' you like a man you hear me. T-Rock foul. That nigga snitchin' and that shit aint tolerated at all. Now what I'm sayin' is T-Rock gone get handled aight. Just back up off my aunt and them and T-Rock's baby mama. They shouldn't be involved in that shit like that you hear me. I understand ya'll young niggas out there active in the streets, but man to man, I'm askin' you. Just lay off my aunt and them."

"How do I know that nigga gone get what he deserve?" Los asked as he pulled on the square.

"Nobody escapes karma, you hear me. You got court next week, right?" Los nodded. "I bet you he won't be there. Just give my fam a pass aight." Gino said before heading back over to the truck. Los never took his eyes off of him while he walked to the Benz.

"Who the fuck was that?" Ace asked as Los handed him his bottle. "T-Rock's cousin."

"What was he talkin' about?"

"Some weird shit, like he gone handle T-Rock. So lay off his aunt and shit cuz you know we been shootin' they shit up like every night."

"Well, what you think?" Los took one last pull on the cigarette an flicked it before replying.

"I don't know my nigga. I really don't know." They posted up and watched Gino and the other mystery man leave the parking lot before hopping in the Benz and going their own separate way.

Chapter 22

William Archebald and David Newman both worked at the same law firm and when William got a call from Alabaster requesting his assistance he instantly agreed. They had done so much business together throughout the years that Alabaster was basically the reason William's kids were able to attend prestigious universities instead of community colleges. Archebald was a vet with the law shit. He was very sharp witted and had an exceptionally high IQ, so he knew how to get muthafuckas to panic during cross examination.

When he took Los' case he instantly went to work trying to find a weak link in the prosecution's case. It didn't take a lot of digging to find out that the whole case was weak. It was all based on one person's testimony. T-Rock's. No guns were found. No surveillance footage. No witnesses. Just the word of a convicted felon and a known drug dealer. When William saw the specifics he knew that he could get the whole thing dismissed.

Because William was Los' attorney, he couldn't represent Jay, so he put Jay in the game with David Newman. He was a young up and coming player at the firm and he had the makings to be a partner one day, so William kept him close. They worked diligently on the case and by the time the preliminary hearing popped up they were more than ready to dismantle whatever the state tried to throw their way.

William and David assured Los and Jay that they had nothing to worry about, but Los was still shitting bricks. It was his first time just being in court like that, so he didn't know what to expect, but Jay was too cool for school. He strolled into the courtroom with a fresh taper fade and a black Armani suit like he was the freshest nigga on the planet and Los showed up looking like he was on his way to the club, rocking some black Roe-A-Wearjeans, a black tee with his iced out cross hanging from his neck, and a black STL fitted cap.

It was supposed to be a private hearing, but the courtroom was still packed. Los instantly noticed T-Rock sitting way in the back wearing a sling on his right arm. All around were his family; mama, sister Cynthia, his cousin Gino and a couple other people who could burn in hell for all Los cared. Their side was deep though. Alabaster came through with a couple of his guys. Ace, his moms, Denise and a couple of her homegirls. Some of Jay's people and a couple faces Los didn't recognize.

But one face Los did recognize. The yellow bone he had fucked in the parking lot the night all that shit happened. He racked his brain trying to figure out why she was there and when she saw him looking her in she smiled and winked at him. Los just nodded and walked over to the table where William and David were talking. "What's up man, we good?" Los asked as they shook hands.

"If everything goes according to plan they should dismiss the bogus charges today. Don't worry, just let us handle this." William said as he patted Los on the shoulders. It sounded convincing, but Los was wondering what would happen if T-Rock got up on the stand and started spilling the beans. When the judge came out the first person they called to the stand was Detective Keith Winburn.

The DA was a very attractive blonde with no ass and enough titties to breast feed all of Angelina Jolie's kids. When she started to ask the DT questions, William leaned over and explained the situation to Los. They had no real viable evidence, so that's why the DA was having people get on the stand. After the detective finished painting an ugly picture of Los and Jay the judge asked William and David if they wanted to cross examine him. They both declined.

Then the DA called T-Rock to the stand. He avoided everybody's eyes by staring at the floor as he approached the bench. Los wanted to kill that nigga so bad that it was ridiculous. He just shook his head and took a deep breath as T-Rock took his seat. He took the oath then the DA instantly started hammering him.

What is your name? Where were you the night you were shot? Where were you before then? Who was with you? Were you under the influence of any narcotics or alcoholic beverages? He mumbled and stuttered as he answered those questions, but when the million dollar question was asked everybody in the courtroom held their breath.

"Did you see who shot you and killed your friends Mr. Arnold?" T-Rock looked at the DA, then at Gino, Los and Jay, then he put his head down.

"Uh no .... no I didn't see who shot me." He mumbled bringing the courtroom to life with outrage and relief. The judge slammed his gavel down a couple times.

"I will have order in this court." He looked back at the DA. "You may proceed Mrs. Jones."

"Think back to that night. You told detectives that you knew the two assailants. That you went to school with the perps who shot you. Then you gave them the defendant's names. Did you not do that?"

"Yea, I .... "

"So, why are you changing your story all of a sudden?"

"It was real late when I got shot. I was drunk and I was high and it was dark out.. .. "

"So, why would you give the detectives both of the defendant's names?" She probed.

"I don't know. I was under the influence. I don't even remember." The DA shot Los and Jay a wicked look before approaching the judge.

"Your honor, this witness has been coerced. Something isn't right." The judge looked at her like, "what the hell do you want me to do about it".

"Continue your line of questioning or turn him over for cross examination."

"But your honor..... II

"Mrs. Jones, we haven't got all day. My docket is quite full and I have to make it to my daughter's dance recital tonight, so if you would please continue or turn your witness over for cross examination." The DA backed away from the judge and stormed over to her table.

"No further questions."

"Mr. Archebald, would you like to cross examine the witness?" The judge asked.

"No your honor. I would like to call my own witness

to the stand. A Miss Athena Witmore." William said as he stood up.

"Alright, but make it quick."

"As quick as I can." Los and Jay mugged T-Rock as he got off of the stand, but everybody in the courtroom including the judge watched intently as Athena took his place. Los just sat there still puzzled by why the fuck she was there. William approached her, made her take the oath, then went into his casual line of questioning.

She introduced herself. Told the court that she was a 23 year old mother of one that worked at a strip club called "The Pink Slip" and she didn't have a single blemish on her record. After her credibility was established, William dropped the question on her.

"So where did you meet the defendants, Ms. Witmore?"

"At the club. I was with some of my homegirls and we seen them ballin', so I introduced myself and the rest is history."

"The night you met Mr. Sims, it was a special occasion wasn't it?"

"Yea. He told me it was his birthday. Or somebody did, I can't remember."

"Of course, I know you heard about the tragic incident that occurred at the Shell gas station two blocks away from the club you were attending?" Athena nodded her head. "Now, to your knowledge is there any way that the defendants were involved in that?"

"No way. That's impossible." Los and Jay looked at each other surprised as soon as the words left her tongue.

"How is that impossible, Ms. Witmore?"

"Because Mr. Simms and Mr. Finch were both with me that night." "Care to elaborate for the court?"

"We met in the club probably around midnight and hit it off, so we kicked it. Then there was a shooting in the parking lot and I got scared, so I asked if they would take me home. They took me home and we ended up having sex." She lied.

"You had sex with both of the defendants?"

"All night. They didn't leave till about six in the morning. No breaks, so there is no way they did what they're being accused of." William turned to the judge.

"Your honor, it should be apparent by now that these charges are bogus and that this case is asinine. The prosecutor has no murder weapons, forensic evidence or eye witnesses and to top it all off my clients have an alibi. There is nothing here linking these two young men to what happened in the parking lot of that gas station. But their faces have been plastered on the news and in the newspapers and their reputations have been sullied."

"Objection, your honor .... " Mrs. Jones stood up.

"No, Mrs. Jones. Mr. Archebald is right. You have no case against these young men and it's obvious. There is nothing there. Sorry." He picked up his gavel and banged. "Case dismissed." Los and Jay jumped up and hugged each other and then shook David's hand. He got paid for nothing because he didn't even have to do shit. William walked over and shook Los' hand with a proud smile.

"I told you not to worry."

"Yea, you did. Usually when people say that it makes you worry even more."

"Well, it's over now. Just don't catch anymore murder cases because everything isn't this easy. You guys are either really innocent or really lucky, but I don't want to know which." They shared a quick laugh.

"What's up with Amaya?"

"She goes back to court next week and I think she's going to sign for that two. If she does, she'll be out in about six months. So right now that's what we're pushing for."

"Aight man. Handle my girl right."

"Believe me. I will." When Los turned around Denise and her homegirls were hitting him with a look like, "you got some explaining to do." Los walked over and tried to give her a hug, but she shied away.

"Uh-uh Los. Who is that bitch?" Denise asked pointing towards Athena, who was talking to Jay and the lawyers.

"That's the bitch that just saved me and the homie's ass. What you on?"

"She up there talkin' about ya'll was fuckin' all night and shit." Sharee, Denise's homegirl added.

"First off, mind your own fuckin' business." He said pointing at her. "Second, even if I did fuck that bitch, it was before we got serious, so what difference do it make. Quit lettin' your miserable ass homegirls fill your head with bullshit." Los said as T-Rock and his entourage filed out of the courtroom. They made eye contact and Los raised an imaginary pistol and pulled the trigger. Denise grabbed his wrist and pushed his hand down.

"Leave that nigga alone before he really go and tell on you."

"Next time, aint gone be nobody left to testify."

"Next time? Nigga is you crazy? You just barely beat this bullshit and you talkin' about next time." She quipped.

"Aye baby chill."

"Don't aye baby me. I'm outta here and I don't wanna see you till you get your fuckin' thoughts straight."

"Denise." She snatched up her purse and was about to leave when she heard a feminine voice saying her man's name.

"Hey Carlos." Los and Denise both turned around at the same time to see Athena standing there with her kool-aid grin on.

"What up." He said nervously as she gave him a

hug. She was looking and smelling detectable and all Los could think about was how she put it on him that night in the car. He had to quickly pull away from her as blood started to rush to the tip of his dick. "This is my girl. .... "

"Fiance', Denise." She said shaking Athena's hand with a fake ass smile plastered on her pretty face.

"Fiance'? Well Denise, you are certainly a lucky woman aren't you?"

"Yes, I am. And with this case out of the way we can just look forward to having our first child in peace."

"Yea, and I appreciate you doin' what you did too. That was real official. You hear me." Los cut in.

"It a int nothin', lil daddy. I mean if ya'll really did do that shit I wouldn't want to be the bitch up there testifyin' against ya'll I just try to avoid creating enemies and make friends where I can make friends."

"I can dig it. You got a pen?" Athena went into her purse and pulled out a pen and a little piece of paper. Los wrote down his number and gave it to her. "Look, if you ever need anything hit me up, aight." That's my number, so either Ima answer or baby here gone answer."

"Ok. I appreciate that."

"Naw I appreciate you." Los said before giving her a hug. When they left the courtroom Denise was all over him.

"So you just gone give the little stripper bitch your number right there in front of me like I aint shit, huh? Ya'll flirtin' and carryin' on like I wasn't ever standing there."

"Come on D. you know it wasn't even like that. A nigga fuckin' owe her for getting' my ass outta that sling. You just want a reason to be mad."

"Yea aight Carlos. Let me find out you fuckin' that bitch. I'm a cut your Lil' dick off. Think I'm playin'.

"Whoa. You got some serious mental issues." He said shaking his head. He loved Denise and everything, but he had charted into foreign territory with the relationship shit and he didn't understand how niggas put up with their main squeeze. In his eyes bitches should be grateful that they got the top spot because all the jealousy, accusations and shit talking would get them dismissed in a heartbeat.

Chapter 23

Los spotted the potential in Athena right off the flop, so when she called him a few days after the court date he was at her throat like a wild beast. She was jocking hard because she knew what Los was about. That money. His swag was just unmistakable. At first she thought he was going to trick on her, but she soon found out that, that wasn't going to happen. Athena had mad game herself, so she could smell a trick nigga a mile away and Los just wasn't one of those niggas.

He stayed in her ear something fierce and every time he was around her he made sure she knew he was knee deep in the game, so he kept her mind captivated, but when Los went to swing at the 92 mile an hour pitch he made sure he knocked it out of the park. Athena had a vicious sex game and she was one of those bitches that knew she was bad, so she thought she was the shit.

To the average nigga she was, but to Los she was a wild beast that needed to be tamed and trained. So that's what he did. Got inside her head and force fed her a fantasy then went so hard in between her legs that he had Athena telling herself she loved him. And a couple orgasms later she was screaming that shit at the top of her lungs.

Athena was the type of woman that seldom fucked for free. She had a two year old daughter to take care of, so she had learned how to milk niggas for money, but she couldn't get shit out of Los and just couldn't stop fucking with him. One day when Los swung through, Athena was sitting in her dining room with two other bitches. Obviously strippers and from the way they were staring him down they were obviously open to a session of, "let's fuck a stranger".

"Los I need to talk to you." She said as she got up from the table. Los looked at her and shrugged nonchalantly.

"So talk." She looked at her homegirls for some type of support, but from the look on their faces she could tell that she was alone.

"We've been chillin' for a minute .... "

"No we haven't. I've only known you for like a month."

"Well, you come over here and kick up your feet and fuck me whenever you want, but not once have you offered to help with the groceries or my rent."

"Aight, first off Lil' mama, you need to pump your breaks." Los pulled out a fat stack and held it in front of Athena's face. The two bitches at the table sat there with their eyes gf ued to the wad of cash. "Wasn't none of this shit give to me. My blood, sweat and tears went into accumualtin' this here stack and many more just like it. I got niggas decayin' in the fuckin' ground right now, niggas locked up right now. Just for this. And you want me to offer you somethin' I risk my life to get just cuz I fuck you?" Los stuck the money back in his pocket as he shook his head with a smug little grin. "Naw baby I don't get down like that."

"I was.... I was just sayin…"

"You don't have to say nothin' cuz I completely understand where you comin' from. But I aint that type of nigga. I know that you do what you gotta do and I can dig it, but I aint just gone be givin' nobody no money for no reason. Especially not cuz we fuck here and there. It's a beautiful experience and everything mama, but I aint never notice no price tag on your pussy. What I can do though, is put you on if you tryna get a stack like this." He said patting his pocket.

"What are you talkin' about? Dope?" Los just stared at her like she was stupid. "I don't know. I haven't ever messed with that shit before."

"Lucky for you I teach a crash course. Crack Cocaine 101. You interested?"

"If she aint, I am." One of the strippers spoke up from the table. She was little dark skinned chick, with some extra'd out weave and big titties. Los looked over at her with raised eyebrows.

"What's your name?" "Jewel."

"And you strip at The Pink Slip too?"

"Yea, I'm the one who got these two heifers hired over there." Los looked at the other stripper. She was his age if not younger, caramel skin tone, petite with a beautiful innocent looking face.

"And, who are you?"

"Simone." She answered in a soft feminine voice.

"And you be gettin' down too?" She nodded her head as she smiled nervously at him. Simone was wearing a short Boston Celtic's jersey dress with a pair of white stilettos and Los instantly peeped that they weren't name brand. "How yo pockets doin' lil mama? You straight?"

"I guess I am. There's always room for improvement,

though."

"Yea, I think I wanna do somethin' with ya'll, but first I gotta see ya'll do ya'll thing at the club. Look some shit in."

"Why not come through tonight. It was supposed to be my night off, but I'll go in if you say you're comin'. Athena said.

"Aight, I guess I'm chillin' at the strip club tonight then."

****

Los, Ace and Jay walked into the strip club looking like money, so it only made sense that most of the girls on the floor gravitated toward them. They went and posted up at a vacant table, ordered a couple drinks and Los peeped the scene. A couple strippers offered to give him a lap dance, but Los shot them down and paid for Ace to get a few. He was chilling, but he was really there on business and to show his nigga a good time. It was the first time he had been out with Ace since he got out of the hospital.

Jay was gone off some ex-pills, so he was in his zone popping p's at every bitch that walked past and Los and Ace just sat there getting tipsy and watching the show. The first girl Los noticed was Simone. She was rocking some see through fish net get up shaking her ass in some nigga's face. She definitely wasn't the nervous young tender that was sitting in Athena's dining room earlier that day because she was over there acting like she knew exactly what she was doing.

Los just looked her in and told himself that he'd have to see what she was talking about later on in the third. He continued to scan the floor with his eyes and quickly spotted Athena and Jewel both doing their thing. Jewel had been dancing for the same nigga for about thirty minutes, but Athena had serious fans. Niggas flocked to see her dance and she took advantage of the crowd. Ace saw what Los was looking at and leaned in closer to him, so Los could hear him over the loud music.

"Aint that the bitch from the court house?"

"Yea, that's her." He replied as he pulled on his Newport. "So that's why you dragged me out here?"

"It really aint. I brought you here cuz I'm tired of you sittin' around doin' nothin' with yourself and this muthafucka is like a million dollar spot."

"How you figure?"

"Look around nigga. It's a fuckin' strip club. X, coke and dodi will move like hot cakes in this bitch. And that bitch." Los said pointing to Athena, "and her homegirls is the ones that's gone move that shit for a nigga. I been on some bullshit, sittin' in the spot when I really aint got to no more. I'm hood on all that shit. Been there, done that. It's time for me to elevate my game, ya dig?"

"Hell yea, I can dig it. I was thinkin' about that shit too. And there's a couple lil niggas on my block that act like they hustlin'. I been contemplatin' puttin' them on."

"I don't see why not. I would. Just to see what they produce cuz we aint gotta sit in no fuckin' spot no more if we don't want to. I look at it like this my nigga, you still makin' money even if somebody else makin' it for you.

Amaya taught me that shit."

"Huh, what's up with baby girl anyway?"

"She straight. You know a nigga gone hold her down and she just signed for two years, but she'll be out in a couple months."

"What you gone do when she gets out? Denise aint gain' for none of that so called pimp shit."

"My nigga, that's the last thing on my mind. Ima deal with that when the time comes, but right now, I'm tryna lock these stripper bitches all the way in." Ace and Los looked up and saw that Jay was gone.

"Where the fuck Jay go?" Ace asked no one in particular as his eyes searched the floor.

"Man, there he go right there." Los pointed Jay out. He was trying to climb up on the stage with no shirt on and a hand full of money. They got up and headed that way when they saw three bouncers running towards the stage. One of the big ass steroid junkies grabbed Jay and snatched him off the stage like he was a rag doll. Jay tried to snatch away, but dude had him in a vice grip, so he tried to swing on the bouncer and the nigga put Jay in a full nelson.

"You better calm down lil nigga before I break yo muthafuckin' ass in half."

"Nigga get off me!!" Jay yelled as he squirmed and tried to get loose. "I'll serve all three of you fuckin' muscle bound faggots!" One of the other bouncers grabbed Jay's legs and lifted them off the ground like they were about to carry Jay to the exit, but Los and Ace were up on them in confrontational mode.

"Aye! I know you muthafuckas better put my homeboy down." Los said getting on one. His burner was in the car, but he had snuck in his brass knuckles and he was itching to use them shits. Plus, Los was a fighter on his own, but he always felt ten feet tall with Ace around. The third bouncer approached Los and Ace like he was built of brick or something.

"Move around little man." He commanded in a deep booming voice.

"Nigga you better get out my fuckin' face before it get ugly for you!" Los spat sizing the monkey nigga up.

"Wait! What's gain' on?" Athena asked as her and a couple other half naked beauties got in between them.

"These faggots fuckin' trippin' with the homie." Los said pointing at Jay who was still struggling to get free. Athena turned towards the bouncers who were holding Jay.

"Chad cut them some slack. They're with me."

"This one was tryin' to climb up on stage."

"Ok. He was feelin' himself. It won't happen again, so put him down. Please." Chad looked at her like he was thinking about it then nodded towards the other bouncer to let him go. "Thank you." She said exasperated.

"One more incident and you're all gone." The bouncer that had Jay's legs said pointing at Jay, Los and

Ace. Los hit him with the stale face and flipped him the bird. They ignored the gesture and kept it pushing. Ace looked at Jay and lightly slapped him in the back of his head.

"Go fuckin' put your shirt back on nigga."

"I'm glad that you could finally make it." Athena said sarcastically. "I didn't think you were going to show up."

"I told you I was comin'. Aye this is my nigga Ace and you know Jay." Athena shook Ace's hand as Simone and Jewel walked over.

"So what do you think?" Jewel asked waving her hand around.

"I don't fuckin' like this joint, but I see a lot of potential." He said glancing at Simone.

"Ooooh, who is this?" Jewel asked pushing up on Ace.

"This the homie Ace. Ace that's Jewel the big tittied stripper." Once Los had Ace plugged in with Jewel he took Athena and Simone to the bar and bought them a couple shots. He ran his little plan down to them and without the slightest form of hesitation, they went for it. All they wanted to do was make some extra money and be in the presence of a young ballin' ass nigga. And they could do both if they played their cards right.

After about twenty minutes of gaming Athena and Simone, Los shot to the restroom to relieve himself. As soon as he walked in he saw a nigga snorting lines of coke off of the counter.

"Yea, this place is a fuckin' untapped gold mine." He thought to himself. Los handled his business and washed his hands and as he was leaving the restroom he ran right back into Simone who was standing there talking to one of the other strippers. When she saw Los she said something to the other girl and they both started giggling.

"What's so funny?" He asked as he walked up on them.

"Oh we were just talkin' about what happened with your homeboy earlier."

"I thought ya'll was over here crackin' funnies on a nigga or somethin'."

"Now why would I do something like that?" Simone asked with an innocent look on her face. Los could tell right then and there that her youthful innocent looks were her venom. Los shrugged his shoulders.

"I don't know, but I'm glad I ran into you cuz I been wantin' to rap with you."

"I'll holla at you later girl. Ima let ya'll talk." The other stripper said finding her cue to leave. Once she was gone Simone looked up at Los and smiled showing off her dimples.

"What's on your mind?"

"How old are you?"

"Twenty-one. Why? How old are you?"

"Nineteen."

"Really? You're only nineteen?" She asked incredulously. "I thought you were at least twenty five, but you're only a baby."

"Yea, I know. That's somethin' I've learned to accept, but I was just wondering if you really know how beautiful you are." Simone blushed before replying.

"Tell me, how beautiful am I." She asked looking him right in the eyes.

"This shit may sound corny, but God had to have taken his time on you. Those eyes, them lips, that flawless body." He said pushing up on her. "Every curve is perfect, even the pitch of your voice is beautiful. I swear I'd die a happy man if I could hear that voice screamin' my name."

"Athena told me you had a girl.. .. "

"I do, but what does that have to do with us experiencing each other? What else Athena tell you?" Simone looked up at him smiling. Without saying a single word she answered his question. Athena told her everything. "See, you got one up on me cuz I aint got nobody to tell me lil stories about you and shit."

"What you wanna know? Ask and I'll tell." She said seductively.

"What's your favorite position?"

"Doggy style."

"Huh. So when you gone let me fuck you doggy style?"

"Damn nigga. You kinda straight forward, don't you think?"

"That's what you can always expect from me mama. Straight up. I don't respect muhafuckas that beat around the bush. I tell it like it is and I wanna fuck you." He said nonchalantly like it wasn't shit. Simone stood there cheesing, digging his approach. For a minute she contemplated creeping off with him right then and there, but she didn't want to seem like she was easy.

"I don't know. You got a girl and then you fuck with the homegirl. I don't think you'll have enough time for me because I'm very demanding when it comes to my sex life."

"Well, when you change your mind just call me aight." He said before turning and walking away. Knowing that she had already fallen for the bait.

Chapter 24

Young Hope

Los kicked Athena, Simone and Jewel down with a half-ounce of soft each and all three of them came back with his money the very next day. He went through Jay and hooked up with his ex-man and copped a thousand pills at $2 a-piece. He slid each of them a hundred pills and another half of blow and let them do their thing.

It was cool because Athena knew Los and his boys were some ill niggas, so there was never any problems when it came to the money. None of them ever came back short or with a sad sob story like you would expect from a stripper. They brought Los his shit, re-upped and went on about their business. The money was so good that Los wanted to kick himself in the ass for not getting involved with the pills in the first place.

He was going to definitely make up for it though. When Los and Jay were posted at the Northwest Inn they ran into a Lil' nigga named Deron. He stayed there with his mother, little brother and little sister and went to Holman Middle School. Los and Jay used to fuck with him. Give him money and shit to run errands or just on GP and Los knew that Deron and his family were doing bad, so he decided to put the nigga on.

Los pulled him up and educated him in the ways of dope boy. He showed him the whip game, then took him and his little brother Percy to the mall and got their wardrobe right. Los didn't want to leave Deron's little sister out, so he gave Deron a couple hundred dollars for her and told him that he'd find out if he didn't give it to her.

It was all love though. Los started Deron out with 28 grams of hard and told him sink or swim. Like Los knew he would, he swam. Deron caught on to the game like he was born to sell dope or something. After copping twice he put his best friend Jerelle on and it didn't take long for them to build a squad of young goons.

At the same time Ace was in U-City on the same shit. Calvin bka 40 Cal, was a thirteen year old aspiring street nigga that stayed up the block from Ace's mama's house. He got his name when he was eleven because he got caught as school with a 40 Cal after getting jumped by a local clique called Low Down. When they saw that he was ready for gun play they backed up off the young nigga with lightning speed.

Like most young niggas in the hood, 40 started out dibbling and dabbling with weed and selling booyah to smokers. Ace knew him because he used to fuck with 40's older sister Sharon. She really wasn't much to look at, but she had an ass like Buffy the body and pumped kids out like octomom. So young 40 stayed in a house with his crack head mama, his sister and all the niggas she brought around and her four kids.

It was ugly until Ace stepped in. He took 40 under his wing and put him up on game. Everybody in the hood started showing 40 love because they saw him with Ace. The big nigga from up the street that got shot in the head and lived. When Ace finally put him on, 40 hurried up and got his boy Trey and his cousin Terry involved.

Since 40's house was basically the spot because of his mother's bad habit, all they did was post up and let the money roll in. The niggas Sharon fucked with were selling dope out of the house, but when 40 and his patnas got on that quickly ended. To say that they were highly unhappy about the situation would be an understatement, but because they knew they were pumping for Ace they left the young niggas alone.

While Los and Ace were taking advantage of and exploiting every avenue possible, Jay was on some bullshit. Because Los had the plug Jay was getting bricks for the low, so he was getting his money on, but not like he was supposed to. He tricked off a lot of money on bitches, jewels and cars. Los had to check him one day when he saw Jay give some thirsty ass bitch ten grand because she said she needed a new car.

Jay was a grown man and Los couldn't really tell the nigga how to manage his money, but he made sure Jay knew that he wouldn't be his safety net. Hell, Los had to get shit prepared for the baby. He bought a black Lincoln MKZ and was having a room built in the loft for the baby that kind of put a dent in his savings. But that's why he grinded. So he would be able to afford the necessities in life. Los promised himself that he would never be one of those people who paid attention to gas prices and sales in the grocery stores.

"Fuck what it cost. Get it if you want it." Was his motto and Denise loved that shit. She really wasn't big on unnecessary spending, but when it came to stuff like the loft or the baby's room she spared no expense. Los didn't care, he just liked to see her happy even though he was sticking his dick in damn near every woman he came into contact with.

As the months went by and Denise's stomach got bigger their relationship grew stronger, but Los continued to do her bad because he was in the streets. He had so many bitches literally throwing themselves at him that he couldn't possibly turn them all down. The one time he did try to get his shit together and stop cheating. He lasted about a week and somehow his main thing n the side ended up being Simone.

Becauses he was pumping for him they saw each other basically every day. She was already digging Los, so it didn't take long for his charm to wear her down. Eventually she gave him a chance and Los thought he was going to dominate her, but all that innocent shit went out the window when they got back to her place. Simone was a beast and Los liked having her around because she reminded him of Amaya. But with all the good shit going on it was only a matter of time before something extra'd out happened.

One day Los and Jay were fucking around and decided to push through on Deron and his boy Jerrelle. They were both young, but they caught on quick. They had only been getting it in for a month or two, but they handled business like they had been seasoned in the game. It was funny to Los, watching the two young niggas get they swag up.

When they got to the room, Jerrelle answered the door.

"What up lil nigga." Los said as they entered the kitchenette. Los walked into the front room and plopped down on the couch next to Deron. He went in his pocket, pulled out a bag of cush, some peach cigarillos and started to craft a masterpiece.

"You must got a sixth sense or somethin'." Deron said as Jay sat down on the other side of him. "We was just finna call ya'll niggas to re-up."

"Huh. What you talkin' about? Give me a figure." Los said as he broke the cigarillo open and gutted it on the table.

"Shit, fuck with me on a four and a half for twelve fifty. Let a nigga wln." Los looked at him.

"I liked how you approached that." He looked at Jay. "You see this nigga tryin' to work his angle my nlqqa?" He asked with a little smirk.

"How could I not see it?"

"You think I should fuck with it my nigga?" Los asked as he sprinkled buds into the empty blunt.

"I don't know. You ever fuck with a four and a half before?" Jay asked Deron.

"Naw." Jay looked at Los.

"He's tryin' to step his game up my nigga. Put him on." Jay looked over at Jerrelle who sat in the chair quiet.

"When you start really playin' with this shit and you upgrade aint no movin' backwards. You don't buy zips at a time no more you buy four and a halfs or better. That's steppin' ya game up you hear me."

"Thanks for the sermon nigga." Los said sarcastically as he finished rolling the blunt. "I aint holdin', so serve this nigga for me. I'll reimburse you."

"Don't worry about it. I got it." Los looked at Deron and nodded towards Jay.

"Give that nigga the money."

"Hold down. I gotta run to the car real quick."

"Aight. Hurry up." Los said as Jay stood up and left. Los lit up the blunt and looked up at Jerrelle. "What you all quiet and shit for? Quiet niggas gotta be watched."

"Naw, I'm just lookin' it in."

"I know what you doin' nigga. I'm watchin' you. Over there all quiet and shit like a weirdo."

"I aint no weirdo nigga." Los waved him off and looked at Deron.

"You up in here grindin' with a lil weird ass nigga and shit." He said as he puffed on the blunt.

"The homie straight. He just be doin' him, just like you do you." Los started laughing and handed him the blunt.

"I like ya'll lil niggas man. I really do, but answer me this. What do you hustle for? What's your purpose nigga?" Without batting an eye Deron replied.

"I hustle to support the fam."

"Pst. That's the modest answer. You sellin' dope. You're riskin' your freedom to get rich nigga. The money is the universal reason I want to know yours. What do you hustle for?"

"I hustle for the money." He said plain and simple. "And I hustle cuz the hustle is in me. Nigga I am the hustle. From now on call me Young Hustle, straight up." Deron popped.

"Shit with a name like that you gone have to go hard. Hustlers hustle from every angle." He replied as his phone started to go off. He looked at the screen and saw Simone's number before answering. "What up."

"Where are you? I need to talk to you."

"So, what's stoppin' you?"

"I need to see you right now, I'm serious."

"Hold up." Los took the phone from his ear and put it to his chest. He looked at Deron and Jerrelle. "Ya'll niggas wanna see some stripper bitches?"

"Hell yea." Jerrelle said getting excited.

"I knew yo lil weird ass was gone say yea first. I'm finna tell this bitch to come over here and if you try to rape my stripper bitch Ima fuck yo lil fuck ass up."

"Man fuck you." Jerrelle yelled as Los put the phone back to his ear. He gave Simone directions to the Inn and posted up chopping it up with Deron and talking shit to Jerrelle. Jay came back and served Deron and another 15 minutes went by before they heard a couple of bangs at the door. Los nudged Deron with his elbow.

"Go get that shit." He looked over at Jerrelle as Deron got up to answer the door. "Can you roll?"

"Yea." He tossed another swisher sweet and the bag of cush in Jerrelle's lap. As he started to roll up a blunt Deron walked back into the front room with Simone and Athena. The first thing Los noticed was that Simone's right eye was black. Then he was the wicked look on Athena's face.

"Fuck happened to you?"

"I happened to her nigga!" Athena spat. "You fuckin' my homegirl Los? That's how you gettin' down?" Los busted out laughing, while Jay, Deron and Jerrelle sat around watching intently.

"Cut it out. You actin' like you my bitch or somethin'. Like you aint know what this was from jump street. Then you got Simone in here with a black eye, probably aint gone be able to work cuz don't nobody want a lap dance from a stripper with a black eye and shit." He said chuckling.

"Yea I knew that you already had a girl or fiance' or whatever the fuck she is. That the first thing I thought about when I found out I was pregnant."

"Pregnant? What the fuck are you talkin' about?" He asked as the smile faded from his face.

"I'm pregnant muthafucka. Shit aint funny now, is it?" Los shrugged with a dismissive flare.

"Actually it is cuz you tellin' me like its mine or somethin'."

"Who's else would it be Los?"

"I don't fuckin' know, but I aint the pappy bitch. Try that shit on anotha nigga, it just might work."

"You really think this shits a game. You know how I found out you was fuckin' my homegirl?"

"I really don't fuckin' care."

"I was the one that took her to the clinic when she found out she was carryin' your child."

"Both ya'll bitches silly." Athena looked at Simone.

"Tell him." She said pointing at Los.

"Los... .I'm ... .I'm pregnant." Simone said timidly.

"Again. Ya'll tellin' me like I give two fucks." He said with his hands palms up. "I suggest you go find your baby daddy's cuz it aint me."

"I can't believe you're sitting there actin like that." Simone said getting emotional.

"Man, I swear to God I seen this episode on Maury, just like this. Strippers and all. This shit is fuckin' crazy." Jay said making everybody bust out in laughter except for Athena and Simone.

"Fuck you Jay!!" Athena spat.

"That's ya problem now, you can't close ya legs. Got damn girl give that poor pussy a break." He cracked, inspiring another bout of laughter.

"Deron, please show these two confused young ladies to the door." Los said in a proper, but mocking manner.

"Burn in hell Los." She yelled before storming off towards the door. Simone stood there with a weird look in her eyes until he shooed her off. When they were both gone Los and Jay looked at each other.

"You got major issues my nigga. Denise is gone fuck you up."

"Get for real man."

"I am for real. You popped on them bitches hard, but you know you been runnin' up in em raw. Look at them bitches. I know I'd be raw doggin' like a muthafucka. Especially Simone. She look like she got some good ....."

"You lustln' nigga."

"I can do that shit. I aint got three baby mamas my nigga. You fucked up and got two stripper bitches pregnant." Jay said busting up laughing. Los couldn't even say shit. He was caught up like Usher.

Chapter 25

It didn't take long for Los to get back in Athena and Simone's good graces. Simone was easy because she had gotten her emotions involved. Los was always popping that shit like he went hard on a bitch and in most cases he did, but when it came to Simone's pretty ass he had a Lil' soft spot. Athena was a different case though. That bitch was angry and the only reason Los could keep her under control was because he had the bag.

Everything seemed like it was on the up and up, but behind closed doors there was a lot of back stabbing going on. After that little episode at the hotel Jay decided to push up on Simone and shoot his shot. She went for it and let him hit and when she saw that Jay would trick on her she made sure he would keep coming back.

They started fucking around on the regular and they were real extra'd out. Like one day Jay popped up at Simone's apartment and she was in there with some other chick. Chillin'. Jay took her in the bedroom and got it in. Head and all. When they were done they went and posted up with the other girl. Not even five minutes later they heard a knock at the door. Simone got up and peeked out the blinds. She turned around and smiled at Jay and her homegirl.

"Watch this." She said as she opened the door. "Hey baby." She greeted Los as she started to tongue kiss him. Jay just sat there wanting to say something. Just a few minutes ago he had his dick in her mouth and there she was swapping spit with his homie. That's just some of the shit they were on together and Los acted like he never suspected a thing. Either that or he didn't care, but Jay was willing to bet it was the former.

One night Jay had just finished putting it to her when his phone started going off. It was nigga that he sold work to requesting a nine piece, so as much as he didn't want to, he had to part ways with his jump off to go make a swerve. It was late, about one in the morning and as Jay headed to his car he peeped a group of niggas posted up across the parking lot.

He thought he recognized a couple of them, but it was too dark to be sure. Jay popped the locks by remote and pulled his pistol from his waist, so all he'd have to do was aim and bust if shit got ugly. The group of niggas stopped talking and all focused their attention on him and the phat iced out chain he wore that glistened underneath the street lights.

"I think that's that nigga Jay." He heard one of them say and his heart started beating like a 15 inch subwoofer. "Yea that is that nigga. On my mama."

"Who dat?" Jay asked as he strained his eyes to make out who was talking. Nobody responded, but Jay instantly went on the defensive when he saw three of the five niggas reaching for their waists and pockets. Jay raised his cannon locked in on one of them and pulled the trigger twice. The hollow tips exploded in the nigga's chest lifting him up off of his feet.

The rest of the niggas scattered, but not before returning fire. Jay started to run back inside, but he wasn't about to get cornered in an apartment, so he broke full speed. He stopped, ducked down behind a white Tahoe and tried to catch his breath. The second the shooting stopped Jay rose up about to get a couple shots off, but he didn't get a chance to. As soon as the shooters saw Jay they opened up again. Two bullets barely missed his face and shattered the windows on the Tahoe.

"Got damn!" Jay said exasperated as he dropped to the ground. "These muthafuckas really tryna kill a nigga." The shooting stopped again and Jay could hear their footsteps as they approached. Jay looked underneath the truck and saw one of their legs and they tried to creep up. Jay closed one eye, aimed and shot the nigga in his leg.

"Ahhhh!!" He screamed out in agony as he fell to the concrete. As soon as he hit the pavement Jay hit him two more times, then scrambled to his feet and took off running while he shot blindly behind him. Even though Jay could barely breath, his will to stay alive kept him on his feet, but because of the lack of oxygen to the brain he started to get sluggish.

Jay posted up behind a red Impala and silence fell on the parking lot. He looked underneath the car and didn't see anybody's feet. He slowly rose up to peek over the trunk of the car and again he didn't see a soul. Jay struggled to catch his breath before making another mad dash for the shelter of another car. As soon as he came from behind the Impala the gun shots resumed.

One bullet tore through Jay's abdomen and another lodged itself in the back of his thigh sending him to the ground.

"Ah fuck!!" He cried out as he blood started to blanket the concrete.

"I got him cuz!" He heard one of them yell as he tried to get up, but he couldn't. His leg felt like it weighed a thousand pounds, every time he moved he felt like he was tearing the wound in his side open and he couldn't fucking breathe. Jay just turned over on his back, lifted his cannon and waited for somebody to come into his line of fire.

One of them emerged from behind a truck and Jay started pulling the trigger, but the gun jammed. He closed his eyes and dropped the burner in defeat as the first nigga walked up on him.

"Look at me muthafucka!" Jay didn't have to. He recognized the nigga by his voice, but he opened his eyes anyway. T-Rock stood over him huffing and puffing with his burner aimed at Jay's head. The other two niggas ran up and instantly started stomping Jay's head and torso. He tried to block some of the kicks and cover up his face, but he was too weak. It was over with and he knew it.

"I know you stupid ass niggas thought it was over, huh?" T-Rock asked when they stopped kicking his ass. Jay just looked up at him seething, trying to suck air into his lungs.

"Suck my dick, faggot!" Jay spat and T-Rock let out a devilish chuckle.

"Nigga suck on this." T-Rock pulled the trigger three times and the last thing Jay ever saw was a flash of light. T-Rock looked at his two homeboys before turning and taking off running.

Chapter 26

The sound of the phone ringing and vibrating across the top of the nightstand woke Los up out of his deep sleep. He looked over at the clock on his digital cable box and saw that it was only 9:12 am. Los let out a frustrated sigh as he rubbed his face and reached for the phone with his other hand. He was tired than a muthafucka because he had gotten in at 5:30 am from a long night of running the streets.

He had made an easy couple of grands which sat on the nightstand next to his pistol and cell phone then he ran into lil jump off that he went to school with. She was a pretty lil Jada Pinkett look alike, so she had always been on the hit list, but Los never really had a chance to get at her. Until that night and Los sprinkled his magic and ended up smashing. The long night was worth it, but the fatigue was kicking Los ass.

"What up." He said as he answered the phone.

"You're a hard muthafucka to catch up with."

"Who dis?"

"Big bro nigga."

"Oh shit. Yea, what up my nigga." Los said as he started to wake up.

"Don't fuckin', oh what up me, nigga. You know I went to court yesterday and didn't nobody show up."

"Awe man. I forgot my nigga. My fault. What they on with you?"

"Guilty on all counts. I go back for sentencing next week."

"You fuckin' serious?" Los asked as he sat up in bed.

"Why the fuck would I be playin'? Of course, I'm serious, but I need you to handle some shit for me."

"Anything."

"Remember that bitch Ava? That dark skinned bitch that stayed with me in Belleville."

"Yea, what's hood?"

"That bitch dipped out with my money. I need that fuckin' money bro, me? I gotta file for this appeal."

"How much?"

"Somewhere close to four hundred racks, no extras. I need that shit."

"Maaaan. Why you trust a bitch with your fuckin' money Vic? That's stupid. I thought you were sharper than that."

"I fucked up and thought I could trust her."

"You a fuckin' weirdo, on my mama. Where the bitch at nigga?"

"The bitch ran to Oklahoma."

"Oklahoma? What the fuck? Man, give me the info, I'll go get your money." As Los went into the drawer on his nightstand and wrote the info down he heard some commotion coming from downstairs. Los said fuck it and decided to get up. When he went downstairs Ace, Denise, Deron, Jerrell and 40 were in the kitchen. Everybody's attention shifted to Los and he could tell by the looks on their faces that something was wrong.

"What's going on?" He asked as he started towards the kitchen. Denise just stood there leaning against the counter obviously on the verge of crying.

"It's Jay man. He got shot last night." Ace said solemnly.

"So where is he? He aight?" Los asked, but in his heart he already knew the answer.

"He's gone my nigga. They fuckin' killed the homie." Los and everybody else standing there knew exactly who "they" were. He wigged out and kicked over the bar stools that sat at the island in the kitchen. He felt sick, nauseated. Los leaned on the island for support and buried his face in his arms. Denise rushed over to console him and after about thirty seconds he finally lifted his head and looked at Ace.

"What happened? I mean where was he?"

"He was over there in Britton. In them apartments yo baby mama stay in." Jerrelle said making everybody look at him. "I mean...... "

"Baby mama?" Denise asked as she pulled away from Los, her facial expression demanding an explanation.

"Naw, I meant to say my baby mama." Jerrelle said trying to correct the situation.

"Nigga please. You aint got no fuckin' baby mama." She looked back at Los. "You got some bitch pregnant on me Los? Is that what you did?"

"Denise, this really aint the time for all that." Ace tried to step in and she turned around and went off on him.

"You probably knew this whole time, you piece of shit."
"Calm the fuck down."

"Bye." She said dismissively putting her hand up in Ace's face as she turned back towards Los. "Who is the bitch? Do I know her?"

"What bitch?" Denise stared at him for a minute before she attempted to land a quick slap. Los swatted her hand away and snatched her. "Fuck wrong with you Denise? You better take yo ass on with that shit!" He said as he pushed her away.

"Aye nigga, watch how you handle my sister." Ace said as he went to catch Denise before she fell.

"You can fuckin' miss me with all that shit nigga. That bitch extra'd out."

"Bitch?" Denise echoed.

"Yea, you got damn right bitch. Try to slap me again and Ima beat your muthafuckin' ass, straight up!" He spat pointing at Denise.

"No the fuck you won't. And you got one more time to call her a bitch nigga." Ace said stepping forward. Los spread his arms and sized Ace up.

"Fuck you gone do nigga? Mind your fuckin' bitness!" Ace hauled off and socked Los square in his jaw making him fall back against the island. He got off a couple more punches before Los could throw his guard up and block some of the shots. He quickly regained his composure and sent a couple hammers Ace's way to back the big nigga up. They sat there in the middle of the kitchen locking like pits damn near going blow for blow.

40 didn't like what he was seeing so he tried to rush Los from the blindside. As soon as he took a step in that direction Deron rocked him so hard that a sharp pain shot up hts right arm. 40 stumbled and Deron and Jerrelle instantly got right on his ass. 40 didn't ball up though. He shook the daze off and held his own. Deren and Jerrelle were beating his ass hands down, but every so often one of them would get caught with one of his wild swings.

The scene was like something straight out of a movie. The shit went on for about a minute before a single gunshot made everybody freeze in their places. They all looked over and saw Denise standing there with one of Los' guns in the air. Barrell still smoking.

"Ace, take me home please." She said with her eyes al watery. "I'm ready to go." Ace backed away from Los gritting on him the whole time. "Come on. Fuck him!"

"Naw fuck ya'll!" Los spat right back.

"Yea, you right nigga." Ace said as he gestured for 40 to come on.

"I fuckin' know I am nigga. I fuckin' built you." Denise pointed the gun at Los. "You better use it bitch." Ace snatched the gun out of her hand, dropped it on the floor and nudged her along to the elevator. Los looked over at Jerrellle and Deren as he wiped some of the blood from his busted lip and shook his head. When Denise, Ace and 40 were gone Jerrelle went and picked up Los' burner and took it to him.

"Say bro, my fault. That shit just came out. I wasn't tryna start nothin'." Los just stood there leaning up against the counter with his arms crossed and a real intense look on his face. He took a deep breath and looked at Jerrelle.

"Get the fuck outta my sight before I do somethin' I regret to you." Jerrelle hurried up and made himself invisible. Deron saw what kind of mood he was in, so he left the kitchen to go talk shit to Jerrelle. Once again, Los had a thousand things on his plate, but Jay's death was so surreal. After Los got out of the hospital Jay was the one that helped him get back on and now he was gone forever. He had a lot of shit to do, but retaliation was at the top of the list.

Chapter 27

That night Los went on a couple solo missions. He rode through and shot a couple houses up and caught a group of niggas at a corner store. He saw one of the niggas that he used to see with T-Rock back in school, so he hit a couple blocks, ejected his spent clip, replaced it with a fresh one, rode back around and gave it up to them niggas.

The next morning Los showed up at Jay's mother's house and gave her a couple grand for the funeral and told her to call him if she needed anything. About a week later they had the funeral and Ace and Denise didn't even acknowledge Los. 40 kept mugging and Deron volunteered to handle the problem, but Los told him to blow it off.

Shit was falling apart left and right. Just a few days before the funeral Vic got sentenced. The fucking scene was disgusting. Los showed up to the Federal Courthouse by himself and saw Vic sitting there shackled down like a wild beast. The judge was a miserable looking old white man and after talking with a couple other white men he got right to business. Vic had been found guilty on all charges and was sentenced to 600 months.

Los sat there doing the math in his head and the shit translated into 50 years. Then after he gave Vic his time the judge had the audacity to say good luck. Vic rose up from the chair and his lawyer tried to say something, but Vic shook him off, walked around the table and approached the judge's stand.

"Fuck luck bitch! 600 months? How the fuck Ima do 600 months you bitch ass fuckin' cracker? You might as well fuckin' kill me right now! You might as well fuckin' hang me you racist pussy!" Vic spat as the bailiffs all rushed him. Even shackled up he was hard for them to subdue. They wrestled Vic down and when they got control of him they roughly snatched him up and carried him out of the court room.

He kept blowing a gasket the whole way out. Los just watched in shock. 50 years was a lifetime and Vic hard to serve that time in what was basically a bathroom with another grown man in it. When Los left he went straight home and got on the computer. With the info Vic gave him for Ava, Los looked her up on yellowpages.com and got her phone number and address. Then using the address Los went on Mapquest.com and printed out a map.

Los went and rented a car, snatched Deron up and hopped on the highway headed for Oklahoma. About twelve hours later they arrived in Oklahoma City and crashed at the Green Carpet Inn. The next morning at the crack of dawn Los and Deron got up and went to the address Ava was listed under. She stayed on the South side, right off of SE 66th. A couple blocks behind a 7/11. As soon as Los pulled on the street he saw Vic's Lac and a silver Denali sitting in the driveway.

"Jackpot." Los said to himself as they drove past the house. They made the block a couple times, looking shit in before going to get something to eat. Most of the day they sat parked up the street watching Ava's house and the bitch never left once, but she had a steady stream of traffic. Los was getting restless, waiting for her to leave, so he came up with an idea. As soon as it got dark they were going in whether she was there or not.

When darkness fell on the city Los and Deron got out of the rental and crept up on the house. Los went around back and Deron went straight up to the door and knocked. Ava answered as she put one of her earrings in. She was dolled up and it was obvious that she was getting ready to go out. Deron just stood there staring at the chocolate skinned stallion.

"Who are you?"

"Oh my fault, but damn. You need to be in some videos or somethin'. I swear." Ava stuck her head out the door, looked around suspiciously then looked back at Deron.

"You lookin' for somebody?"

"Yea, I'm Craig. Is Samantha here?"

"No, you have the wrong house."

"Naw I just called and she told me the house on the corner with the Lac and the truck in the driveway."

"Sorry baby boy, Samantha lied to you because she doesn't stay here. Bye." She said as she started to close the door, but Deron stuck his foot in the way. "What the fuck are you doing?" She asked as she tried to push Deron out of the doorway. The sound of the hammer being cocked on a revolver behind her sent a paralyzing chill down her spine. Deron casually entered the house and closed the door behind him as Ava slowly turned around. When she saw Los tears instantly filled her eyes.

"Oh my God Los please don't." She pleaded with her arms out.

"Where's Vic money?"

"Los please.....I....I..."

"Where the fuck is the money?!" He asked putting the gun to Ava's temple. She shrieked from his outburst then began to cry uncontrollably. "You wasn't fuckin' cryin' when you tried to leave my brother high and dry, so don't be fuckin' cryin' now." He looked at Deron. "Tear this muthafucka up." Deron instantly started trashing the living room looking for the money. The house was plush, so Los could tell that she had really been enjoying Vic's hard earned stacks.

"Los, the only reason I left is because the Feds spooked me. I didn't.. .. "

"I don't wanna hear that shit. Tell me where the fuckin' money is before I splatter yo stupid ass all over this living room." Ava pointed a shaking index finger towards a closet in the dining room.

"The money is in there. All of it." Los looked at Deron and nodded towards the closet. Deron ran over, snatched the door open and started going through everything. "No, there's like a trap door in the floor. The money is down there." Deron snatched everything out of the closet and sure enough, there was a trap door. Deron bent down and pulled it open. It wasn't deep. Just about two feet or so, but Deron didn't see anything, but dirt.

"That bitch lyin'. Aint nothin' down here."

"It's down there, I swear to God it is." She said in a panicky voice. "You just gotta reach around and feel for it." Los grabbed her by her throat and shoved her into the dining room.

"Get that shit then." Ava walked over to the closet,

looked at Los, then hesitantly got on her knees. She stuck her arm down through the trap door and felt around for the fire proof lock box with the money in it. When Ava found it she fingered the nine millimeter that sat on top of it and contemplated making her move, but when she glanced up at Los again and the fat barrel he had aimed at her head she though twice.

She knew that Los wouldn't hesitate to blow her shit off, but maybe if she gave him the money he'd let her live. She didn't need what was in the safe. She had a cool house, two fresh whips and her jewelry collection was worth at least a hundred grand alone, if not more. Ava put the gun down and pulled the lock box from underneath the house.

"Hold this bitch down." Los said as he picked the black box up and carried it to the table. Deron pulled his pistol and pointed it at Ava. On the outside he looked like he was straight, but on the inside Deron's stomach was in knots. He had never shot anybody or anything like that and he really didn't want to. Especially not a woman, but for some reason he just knew that Ava's grave stone would have her birth date and that day's date on it. "Where's the key?"

"On my key ring hanging up by the door." She said as tears rolled down her cheeks ruining her make up. Los went and got the keys then went to work trying to find the key that fit. When he found it, he unlocked the box and opened it. He looked back at Ava with an 'I can't believe this shit' look on his face.

"What the fuck is this?"

"That.. ... that's the money." Los turned back to the box and eyed the stacks adding shit up in his head.

"This is only like a hunnet and twenty grand. Where the fuck is the rest of it? Vic told me it was four."

"That's everything right there." Los snatched his gun up off the table and walked over to where Ava was sitting on the floor. Deron saw the situation about to get ugly, so he got the fuck out of the way. Los cocked his arm back and slapped the shit out of Ava with his burner.

"Where the fuck is the rest of the money?!" He exclaimed making veins pop out of his neck. Ava sat there balling as a steady stream of blood fell from her mouth. Los cocked his arm back again and Ava quickly sat up with her arms up in a pleading manner.

"Wa.... wait.. ... wait.. .. please Los stop!! Please! I spent it. I spent the money. Please don't kill me. I don't wanna die." As those words rolled off of her tongue the front door came open and everybody shifted their attention in that direction. A nigga wearing an orange shirt and an A's fitted cap walked into the house and instantly froze in his place when he saw what was going on.

"Close that door." Deron said as he ran up on the nigga. The stranger closed the door and put his hands up.

"What the fuck is going on?"

"Shut the fuck up." Deron said as he peeked out the window to see if there was anybody else coming. Los was too busy watching Deron and the kid nigga to notice Ava reaching for her pistol through the trap door. When Los looked back at her, she had the gun in her head. She quickly raised it and tried to get a shot off, but Los kicked the gun out of her hand causing it to discharge.

Deron took his eyes off of the kid nigga to see what

happened and ol boy tried to make his move. He grabbed Deron's wrist and tried to wrestle the gun out of his hand as Ava crawled into the living room. Los raised his cannon and shot Ava in her back twice. She crumpled to the floor as blood started gushing from her wounds.

He raised the gun and tried to get a clear shot off at the kid nigga, but Deron was in the way.

"Move!" Los yelled as he continued to look for a shot. The kid nigga saw what Los was on, so he tried to keep Deron in front of him to act as a human shield. Deron head butted the nigga dead in his shit breaking his nose then he ran his knee into his groin.

"Ahhhh!!" The kid nigga groaned out in pain. He fucked up and let go of Deron's wrist to grab his nuts. As soon as Deron got his hand free she put the gun to the kid nigga's chest and blew four fat craters in his shit. He fell back up against the door and slumped over in the corner, his lifeless eyes wide open. Deron stared at the body in shock then looked back at Los like 'what did I just do.'

"Come on my nigga. We gotta shake." Los said as he went back into the dining room and got the lock box off of the table. They ran out the sliding glass door, Los had snuck in through, got in the rental and hit the highway. Los looked over at Deron and could tell he was feeling fucked up about laying the kid nigga down. It was ugly, but it was just another part of the game. "You aight?"

"Man. I don't know. I aint never kill nobody before Los."

"It was either you or him my nigga. You can't dwell on that shit cuz you did what you had to. I liked how you handled yourself though my nigga. You know how to operate under pressure."

"That a int no shit I could get used to."

"I been in the mix for a minute my nigga and I aint used to that shit. Probably never will be, but all that matters is that when it all boils down you don't hesitate to pull that trigger. I wouldn't have brought you with me if I didn't think you were ready nigga. Murder is a part of the game straight up. I don't like that shit, but it is what it is. It was like this before you, me and the niggas over us. Don't get bent outta shape about it."

"I aint. It just got me feelin' weird and shit. Seein' dude dead like that, but you right. It was him or me."

"Exactly. Now quit cryin' and use this shit to elevate your game Lil' nigga. I need a real thoroughbred to pass the torch to."

"I'm as thorough as they come nigga."

"Yea we gone see muhafucka."

Chapter 28

When Los got home he counted the money up and that shit came to one hundred and twenty five thousand on the dot. He couldn't believe that Ava had actually spent three hundred racks. Los waited for Vic to call and when he finally did he told his bro that he had went and retrieved the funds. He didn't have to go into detail because Vic knew what it was. He was salty when he found out how much he had left, but he quickly got over that shit.

There were niggas in there who he was locked up with that had touched millions and didn't have two cents on their books, so he was thankful for everything he had. Vic plugged Los with his attorney and had him drop fifteen grand in the white man's lap. All Los could think was that for fifteen racks Vic should be released.

Los continued to do his thing and as the months passed, Athena and Simone blew up. With their stripper careers paused because of the pregnancies Los had to find something else for them to do. He started having them make swerves for him. A nigga would call trying to cop a four and a half and Los would send one of them.

Even if they did get pulled over, who would fuck with a pregnant woman. Fucked up or not Los refused to deal with a female if she didn't pull her own weight. One night Los was laid up at Athena's apartment when his phone started going off. He rolled over and was trying to ignore it, but Athena picked it up and answered.

"Hello." Los looked at her and snatched the phone from her ear.

"What the fuck I tell you about that shit?"

"I don't care about none of those little bitches you be

talkin' to nigga. If that's what you trippin' about."

"Shut up." He said as he put the phone to his ear.

"Who is this?"

"This is Rachel."

"Oh, is everything alright?" Los asked sitting up in bed.

"No baby. Denise is in the hospital. Something happened and she went into premature labor."

"What? Is she alright?"

"We don't know anything yet, but I really think you need to be here right now."

"I'm on my way." Los hung up, got out of bed, threw his clothes on and smashed without saying shit to Athena. He jumped in the Benz and sped through traffic until he got to the hospital. When he walked into the waiting room it was packed. Rachel and a couple of her friends, Ace and his young goons, a couple females and two detectives. They were trying to talk to Ace and Rachel, but it was obvious that they were getting nowhere. Rachel walked over to Los and wrapped him up in a warm motherly hug.

"I'm so glad you came."

"What happened? Is she aight?"

"The doctor told us that they were going to have to do an emergency C-section. That was thirty minutes ago."

"What happened?" He asked looking Rachel in the eyes.

"Who are you?" One of the detectives asked.

"Who the fuck are you, punk?" Los spat sizing the jake up.

"Los, no. He's just doing his job." Rachel said putting a hand on Los' chest. She turned to the detective. "This is the baby's father."

"Oh well, you're girlfriend was involved in a shooting." The other DT said.

"A shooting? What are you talkin' about? Did Denise get shot?"

"No, but the car she was riding in, along with this gentleman here did receive a barrage of bullets." The DT said gesturing towards Ace. "I assure you, we will find whoever did this."

"Of course, you will." Los said sarcastically. He looked over at Ace as he headed for the door. Ace gestured for him to come on and Los followed him out. They went outside and Ace lit up a Newport. "What the fuck happened?" Ace took a long hard drag and exhaled the smoke before replying.

"That nigga T-Rock caught me slippin' with my lil sister in the car. He shot my shit up at the stop light and I guess the stress or fear or whatever made Denise's water break." He said as he hit the cigarette again. Los leaned back up against the wall and thought about the nigh him and Jay had got at T-Rock and his cousin at that gas station. Why did that gun have to jam up?"

"That nigga is a fuckin' dead man walkin'." Los said punching his left palm. Ace looked at him as he blew smoke out of his nose.

"Shit aint been the same since Jay died man. You know we all we got my nigga and it took this shit happenin' for me to realize that. We gotta fuckin' kill that nigga homie, straight up. That faggot gotta go."

"On my mama he got it comin' my nigga and I gotta apologize for that shit with Denise...."

"Aint no need for an apology bro. I was there, I seen what happened and I woulda been a bitch nigga if I woulda just stood around and did nothin'. We family Los, shit happens."

"I'm just sayin'."

"Well what's understood don't need to be explained."

"That's right." Los said as he shook Ace's hand.

"Ace." They both looked up to see 40 walking out of the building. "Aye the doctor in there talkin' you your moms right now." Ace flicked his cigarette butt into the parking lot and they ran back to the waiting room. Rachel was standing there listening intently to every word the doctor said.

"Is Denise and the baby aight?" Los asked as soon as they walked in. The doctor turned to him, Ace and 40 and smiled.

"Everything is just fine." He assured him. "But

because the baby was born prematurely, her lungs weren't fully developed, so we'll have to keep her here for a few weeks because she needs the assistance of a respirator in order to breathe."

"What?" Los asked, about to blow up.

"Besides that, the baby is perfectly healthy, so I'm sure that after a few weeks of steroid treatment and close observation she should be ready to go home."

"Can I see her?"

"Let me go and check it out real quick. I don't want to tell you yes or no right now, but I'll see what I can do." When the doctor left everybody sat or stood around awkwardly in silence. About ten or fifteen minutes later the doctor reappeared and led them to the hospital's nursery. The doctor didn't need to point the baby out because she stood apart on her own.

Besides the fact that she was hooked up to a thousand and one machines, she was beautiful. Small and beautiful. Los' baby girl. As he stood there and stared at the frail child all sorts of emotions struggled to break through to the surface. He always thought of himself as a grown man, but it was really time to man up. He had to raise another human being, but before he could fully commit himself, he had to tie up a loose end.

****

When Denise's eyes finally fluttered open she looked around the hospital room and saw Los standing there staring out of the window. It was pouring down hard outside and she could hear the thunder as it vibrated the sky. Los just happened to turn around and saw Denise looking at him. He walked over to the bed and gently took her hand into his own. She weakly pulled away, but the rejection was strong.

"Where's my mother?" She asked looking around like Rachel would just pop up out of thin air.

"She's at the nursery. How you feelin'?"

"Well, where is Ace?" Denise asked ignoring his question.

"He went to go do somethin'. You act like you aint too happy to see me."

"I'm not. Fuck you."

"Look D. I know I fucked up, but.... "

"Yea you fucked up Los. You got two strippers pregnant man, so go be with those silly bitches. We don't have anything to talk about."

"We got a lot to talk about. We got a beautiful baby girl and even if we aint gone be together Ima still be in the picture."

"I got a beautiful baby girl." She corrected. "I don't need you or your blood stained drug money nigga. Fuck you Los. I hate you!" Los took a deep breath and clenched his jaw in an attempt to bite his tongue.

"So what you gone name her?" He asked trying to change the direction of the conversation.

"Truth." She stated simply. Attitude still in tact.

"How'd you come up with that?"

"You know, I was really twisted about you Los. I knew you were doing me wrong, but I always lied to myself and said that you were what I wanted, but in all actuality you're not. When the truth was exposed that day it make me stop lying to myself about us. I was hurt, so I turned to God and He led me to the book of Ruth. Do you know who Ruth was?" Los just shook his head. He had never read a scripture a day in his life. "Ruth was the most faithful and loyal woman in the Bible. You should read it sometime. Ruth is a beautiful name, but I decided to add the T. Then I looked it up. Sincerity, integrity, reality. That's where your daughter's name came from."

"You really put a lot of thought into it, huh?"

"I put a lot of thought into everything I do Los. I guess except for fuckin' with you. I read one verse and it said 'Don't ask me to leave and turn back. Where ever you go, I will go, where ever you live, I will live. Your people will be my people, and your God will be my God'. It's crazy because at one point those words explained how I felt about you, but now, I fuckin' despise you." Los was about to reply, but the sound of the door opening up behind him made him turn around. Ace walked into the room and smiled when he saw that Denise was up.

"How you feelin' baby girl?" He asked as he kissed her on the forehead.

"Cool I guess. I'm just ready to see my baby."

"She's beautiful, on me. I'm finna go get mama real quick, aight."

"Ok."

"I'll be right back." Ace looked at Los. "Let me holla at you."

"It's on." Los followed Ace into the hallway and chopped it up with him on the way to the nursery. "You find out where he at?"

"Yea, I got lil 40 on him right now. If the nigga move 40 gone call a nigga."

"Well what the fuck you waitin' for? Let's go get this muhfucka." Los said instantly getting amped up.

"I'm finna go tell my mama that Denise up and we outta here. Today is that nigga's last day walkin' this earth. Straight the fuck up."

Chapter 29

The rain was beating down so hard that Los and Ace could hardly see the road, even with the windshield wipers on high. They were in Ace's F-150 and the dark clouds that hovered over the city set the grim tone for what they were about to do. 40 had hit Ace and let him know where T-Rock was. As soon as they hit the block they saw T-Rock and some bitch climbing into an old school.

"There they go right there." Los pointed out from the passenger seat.

"You think I don't see em?"

"I don't what the fuck you seein'. You still doin' the speed limit nigga, punch that shit." Los said as the old school backed out of the driveway. "Where's 40?"

"I told him to skate cuz this shit finna be ugly." Ace said as he pressed down the accelerator. Los sat there, heart pounding, adrenaline pumping as he finger fucked the trigger on his burner. The old school T-Rock was in stopped at the end of the block at a stop sign and was about to turn right when the F-150 plowed into the car from behind.

The force of the impact sent the old school clear across the street where it collided with a tree. Los sat there holding his forehead. When they crashed, he hit his head on the dashboard opening up a small cut along his hair line. He wiped the blood from the cut as he blindly searched the floor mat for his gun. By the time he got his hand around the handle Ace had already shaken off his daze, grabbed the Mossberg pump and started to go out of the truck.

Gun in hand Los stepped out of the F-150 and into

the heavy rain. Ace and Los instantly went to dumping on the old school, shattering its windows and blowing fat holes in its frame, as they slowly approached. When the shooting stopped the driver side door slowly opened and T-Rock struggled to get out. The crash had fucked him up, plus he had caught a couple hot ones.

Los ejected his spent clip and replaced it with a new one as they continued to advance on the car. By then T-Rock had managed to stumble out of the driver seat and into the rain looking like an old drunk. He stood almost completely hunched over staring at Los and Ace with a gun in his hand as they walked up. He tried to raise his cannon, but Los beat him to the punch.

Boom! Boom! Boom! Boom! The first hollow tip hit T-Rock on the right side of his chest making him stumble back and drop the pistol. The second hit him dead center and the other two pierced his upper abdomen setting him down on his ass, hard. When T-Rock fell it was obvious that he was dead, but Los ran up and pumped one into his face just for good measure. Before turning to run back to the F-150 with Ace he looked over and saw the bitch in the passenger seat of the old school with her head sticking out through the windshield. Her lifeless body slumped over the dashboard like a rag doll. Another casualty of the game. They ran back to the truck, started that raggedy muthafucka up and got the fuck out of dodge.

They rode in complete silence as Ace maneuvered through the back streets. Los ran his hand over the cut on his head and looked over at Ace who sat behind the wheel with a confused look on his face.

"You know you're a psychotic fuck. Why'd you crash into them?"

"I did what I had to do to make sho that bitch nigga didn't get away. And It worked. We finally got that muthafucka."

"Yea. We finally got that nigga." He said more to himself than to Ace. It was crazy though. It didn't even feel like it, but he had been into it with T-Rock for almost six years. Six years, two dead homies, and a dead prostitute later, they had finally caught that nigga and put him to sleep. Los would have been happy or a t least relieved, but he knew that a nigga in the streets could never feel relief.

There would always be some wicked turn of events that lurked right around the corner and Los knew to anticipate that shit. Even though the T-Rock chapter had ended that only meant that another one was about to begin.

Chapter 30

Denise sat in the hospital for about three days and a couple weeks later Truth was allowed to go home with her. Los continued to do his thing, but whenever he got some free time he spent it with his baby girl. Every time he looked at her he thought about his mother. He would have given anything to see his mother holding her granddaughter.

Denise wasn't fucked up about letting him see his child, but she literally couldn't stomach his presence. Los thought she was just talking, but she really did hate him. He had always popped like everything was on a bitch and all that shit, but for the first time in his life he had actually gotten his feelings involved and they weren't mutual.

He wanted to be with Denise, but she made it clear that, that wasn't going to happen. It really fucked Los up because he was being denied something he wanted and he dwelled on it for a hot minute. But after a while he got over it. The only reason he wanted to be with her so bad was because he knew she wasn't fucking with him. He was on some typical nigga shit seeking the thrill of the chase.

One day Los was posted over in the Johnny Shields in East St. Louis with Deron and his little brother Percy. He had taken them out there to fuck with his homeboy Hollow. They were sitting up in an apartment betting a hundred dollars a fight on Fight night round 3 and so far Percy had whooped everybody in the spot, so Los just put his money on him.

It was fairly early. About 10 am, but that didn't stop niggas from drinking and smoking like they were getting ready to go to the club or something. Percy had just won his ih straight fight when Los' phone started to go off in his pocket. It
was loud as hell in the apartment, so he stepped outside to

take the call.

"What up, who dis?"

"So you can't recognize my voice anymore? I know it hasn't been that long?"

"Amaya? What up baby, what you on?"

"Well, I was trying to get a ride."

"A ride? You out?"

"Yea. I got out this morning. Didn't you get my letter?"

"Naw." He lied. He had mail stacked up like books back at his loft from Amaya, Vic and T-KO. Los just never took time to read the shit. Every time he got a letter or something he'd just send them a money order instead of writing back. "Where you at?"

"The Greyhound station downtown."

"Bet that. Hold tight, I'm finna come swoop you."

"Hurry up. I wanna see you."

"I'm on my way." Los ran back into the apartment and pointed at Hollow who was on the controllers with Percy. "Aye Hollow, pay my guy so we can go. You know you can't fuck with him."

"Where ya'll goin'? This lil nigga got me down three hunnet dollars." "We gotta go handle some shit. We'll slide back through later on."

"Maaaan. You got this lil nigga in here swindlin' us and shit." He mumbled as he reluctantly gave Percy three crispy hundred dollar bills. They shook everybody up and then left in the Lincoln. When they got into the truck and pulled out of the parking lot, Los looked over at Deron.

"Where we goin'?"

"To pick the homegirl up. This probably the baddest bitch you ever gone see in your life lil nigga."

"Yea right."

"You gone see." When they got to the Greyhound station Los instantly spotted Amaya. She was sitting in one of those hard ass fiberglass chairs talking to some nigga. They were deep in conversation when he walked over and posted up in front of her with Deron and Percy close behind. Amaya looked up and started cheesing as she stood and wrapped him up in a tight hug.

"Oh, I missed you so much." She said as Los stepped back to check her out.

"Damn Amaya, you look good." He said making her blush. Deron and Percy just stood there gawking. She was already thick when she got locked up, but somehow she had managed to add more ass and hips to her frame and still keep a little waist end her hair dropped just past her shoulders.

"Thank you. Who are they? You babysittin'?" She joked pointing towards Deron and Percy.

"Naw. These my lil guys. Deron and his lil brother Percy.

Aye ya'll this is Amaya. The baddest bitch ya'll ever gone meet." After everybody got acquainted they shot to the mall and Los got her some fresh gear. They spent a couple hours on the town catching up with each other then Los took her back to the loft.

"I like what you did with the place. It's a big improvement from what it was when I left." Amaya said as she walked around and checked everything out.

"Yea. You know I'm glad you're back. It seems like forever done past."

"I know and it's only been ten months."

"You aint got no lil sisters or cousins or nothin'?" Deron asked as he plopped down on the couch.

"No, I wish I did though."

"Quit lustin' lil nigga." Los said lightly slapping Deron on the back of the head. He looked at Amaya and motioned for her to follow him into the kitchen. He grabbed a bottle of Gatorade out of the refrigerator and offered her one, but she declined. Amaya sat on one of the bar stools as Los popped the top and took a swig.

"So how's the baby?" She inquired as she leaned forward on the counter.

"She's good."

"What about the strippers you got pregnant?" She asked with a slight smirk.

"Who told you about that shit?"

"Does it really matter? You may not know this, but a lot of people keep your name in their mouths. I heard about everything that's been goin' on with you."

"Huh. Well them bitches straight."

"Why they gotta be bitches?"

"Man, I don't even know if them babies are mine. I just keep them bitches around because they gullible."

"Was you dirty dickin' em?" Los shrugged.

"Maybe a couple times, but….."

"But nothin'. You know them babies are yours nigga. Quit frontin'. I aint even been gone a year and everything is so different. You got a baby, with not one, but two more on the way. Then Jay …. " She said looking down at the counter top trying not to get emotional. It was still hard to believe that he was actually gone.

"Yea. You know we rode for my nigga."

"I knew what was up when I saw that shit on the news. He was lucky to have a friend like you."

"Naw, I was lucky to have a friend like him and a friend like you. A lot of this shit wouldn't have been possible without ya'll, for real." He said as Deron walked into the kitchen puffing on a swisher sweet. He tried to hand it to Amaya, but she shook her head.

"I can't. I have to check in with my probation officer in the morning."

"That's fucked up."

"I know, right. How old are you Deron?"

"Fourteen goin' on thirty." He replied with smoke coming out of his nose. Los could tell that he was digging Amaya because he had his swag turned up a little. "Why, what up?"

"I was just wonderin' that's all." She said as his phone went off. He pulled it out of his pocket and looked at it to see a text message from Jerrelle. Deron read it then looked up at Los with a frown.

"Fuck wrong with you?"

"Jerrelle just said some niggas jumped him at Northwest Plaza."

"That nigga need his ass whooped. I don't like that lil muhafucka." Los said taking another drink from his bottle.

"Man that's the homie. Let me use your car real quick."

"What car?"

"The Benz or the Lincoln. It don't matter."

"You gotta be out yo rabbit ass mind if you think Ima let you push either of them shits nigga."

"Can you drive?" Amaya asked Deron.

"Yea I know how to drive. If you won't let me push then run me up there real quick, so I can see what's up."

"Let him drive the Benz. I'll take responsibility if he fucks it up." Amaya said with a little grin.

"Ya'll are fuckin' crazy."

"Come on Los. Fuck with me." Los exhaled and snatched the blunt from Deron's hand with an attitude.

"You know where the keys at. Fuck my car up and Ima dump you in the Mississippi."

"It's on." Deron bolted from the kitchen and Los looked over at Amaya who had a big smile plastered all over her face.

"That shit funny to you?"

"Kinda." She said as she stood up and walked around the island to where Los was standing. Amaya stood in front of Los staring him in the eyes while listening to Deron and Percy leave the loft. When she was sure they were gone Amaya leaned in and kissed Los. A peck on the lips quickly turned into an intense spit swapping session. Los was at her so tough that it was like he was the one who had just been released from prison.

He went right to work undressing her and she helped him come up out of his shit. When Los got Amaya completely naked he lifted her up onto the counter scanning her flawless body with his eyes. He started sucking on her nipples as she greedily grabbed his swiped and tried to guide him into her. Los grabbed her ass pulling her to the edge of the counter and after a few seconds of struggling he fully penetrated her tight unshaven love nest making her cry out.

Amaya wrapped her legs around Los' waist as he began to give her every inch of him. All you could hear in the kitchen was Los' heavy breathing, Amaya's soft moans and the sound of her gushy being run into repeatedly. Los held onto her juicy ass staring her dead in the eyes as he started to pick up the pace. Trying to touch her soul with every stroke.

"Uhhhl Los right there. Stay right there. That's my spot!" She shrieked out as Los hit it from a left angle. Amaya just held on for dear life, thinking. "Got damn this nigga know what to do with this pussy."

"You like that?" He asked as he began to hit her spot harder.

"Ooooh, Daddy I love it. Ah, ah, I think I'm about to cum!" She screamed out as here entire body started to tremble. Amaya's legs began to shake uncontrollably and a few seconds later Los could feel a warm liquid literally shoot out from between her legs. He looked down and saw Amaya's love juices everywhere.

"Got damn girl." He said as he pulled out of her soaking wet snatch. Los pulled her off the counter, turned her around, bent her over and gently eased back in it, filling her up to capacity. He lifted one of her legs up and began to bury his bone, hitting the bottom of her pit every time he plowed into it. It didn't take long for her to reach another climax and soon afterwards Los unloaded his clip.

Amaya laid sprawled out over the counter top wore

out, breathing like she had just run a hundred yard dash. Los looked over at the entrance of the kitchen and saw Percy standing there with his mouth agape. He had walked into the kitchen for something to drink and ended up catching the peep show of his young life.

Chapter 31

When New Year's rolled around Los was in another place mentally. His game had advanced so much in the past 365 days that it was ridiculous. He wasn't even twenty years old yet, but he had already seen and done shit that niggas twice his age only dreamed about. Money, hoes, cars, clothes. When it came to that type of shit he had a been there done that kind of attitude and he had a right to.

Money was not an issue at all. Los remembered when he first got to St. Louis, people greeted Vic in the mall like he was a celebrity or something. He would have never imagined that just a few years later he would be a certified Star with a wicked reputation in the streets and enough money that he could wipe his ass with ten or twenty racks, flush it down the toilet and not miss it.

And with his bottom bitch back by his side, Los was really feeling himself. He had major love for her, but besides that he had an overwhelming sense of appreciation for Amaya because he knew how instrumental she was in his success. He didn't put her back out there, but because Amaya was Amaya she found a way to pull her own weight.

The situation with Denise was a completely different story. She played more games than a three year old on Christmas. Los spoiled the shit out of Truth, but whenever he'd stop by to pick her up Denise would strain him up. She was always crying about him having her daughter around other bitches, but she didn't waste any time moving in with some nigga she was fucking with.

It was a bunch of bullshit but Los dealt with it because he refused to turn his back on his seed and the kids kept coming. Athena hit him with a two piece. Two baby boys and, a couple weeks later Simone had a little girl. Los hurried up and filed for DNA tests. He wasn't fucked up about paying the five hundred dollars a piece for them. To him it was money well spent.

After about a week or two the results arrived at the loft and all of the babies were his. Four babies, three baby mamas. It was ill, but Los took care of them all. He didn't want his kids looking at him like he looked at Alabaster.

Between taking care of his youngins' and handling his business in the streets, Los barely had real time to himself, so when New Year's popped up he decided to let loose. They went out to the club and Los' entourage took up the whole VIP. They even snuck Deron, Jerrelle, 40 and a couple of their little patnas in and they did it up real proper like. After a long night of lung and liver abuse they decided to shake that mothafucka. It was about 2:45 am when the group of intoxicated hood niggas and hood rats fell out of the club.

Los, Amaya, Deron, Jerrelle and a couple of jump offs got into the Lincoln. Ace, 40, a couple of their guys and some bitches jumped in Ace's Denali and a car full of bitches pulled out of the parking lot behind them. They were all headed to Ace's house to kick it for the rest of the night. Los sat in the passenger seat, eyes so low that it looked like he was sleeping. Amaya pulled up to a red light and looked over at him.

"Los, I know you aint sleep." She said as Ace pulled up on her side.

"Naw."

"Well, I'm hungry. Let's go to the Waffle House or something."

"You drivin'. That's on you mama."

"Hell yea! I'm hungry than a muhafucka too." Jerrelle said sitting up in between the two front seats. He really wasn't. He just wanted a reason to flash his fat knot in front of the two girls him and Deron had managed to knock at the club.

"Quit fuckin' yellin' lil nigga. Fuck wrong with you?" Los snapped gritting on Jerrelle.

"My fault my nigga." He said as he sat back feeling a little embarrassed as Amaya rolled down her window and waved at Ace to get his attention. The nigga in the passenger seat of the Denali rolled down his window and Ace leaned over and nodded.

"What up?"

"Aye, we gone stop at the Waffle House."

"Man I was just thinkin' that same shit, on me. We gone follow ya'll."

"Ok." Amaya said as Los glanced out of his own window. He watched through blood shot red eyes as a black truck pulled up along-side them. He didn't think anything of it until he saw the tinted windows roll down. Los caught glimpse of the driver before he produced an Uzi.

"Get down!!" Los yelled as he grabbed Amaya's head, pushed it down on the middle console and covered it with his upper body. Automatic gunfire erupted from the Uzi's barrel peppering the MKZ with fat holes and shattering the windows.

"Ahhh." One of the bitches in the back seat screamed

out as a stray bullet tore into her flesh. Amaya panicked and floored the accelerator making the Lincoln burn out from the stop light. The shooting persisted as she blindly steered the
SUV.

"Fuckin' wicked!" Los heard Deron yell from behind him. The bitch that had already caught a slug got hit with another stray. This time the bullet slammed into her temple at 95 miles per hour, instantly splattering her shit all over Deron, Jerrelle and her homegirl. When the gun shots stopped, Los heard the truck burning its tires as it made a quick turn.

He let Amaya go and she quickly sat up trying to see where they were going. Los felt a familiar sting in his back and when he reached around his shirt was soaking wet. He didn't even have time to say shit because they were on a crash course with some parked cars. Amaya knew that if she hit the brakes the truck wouldn't stop in time, so she rotated the steering wheel all the way to the left in an attempt to make a hard turn.

It probably would have worked if they weren't going so fast, but the truck lifted up on two wheels and performed a tumbling act in the middle of the street. It flipped about three times before coming to rest upside down. Within seconds Ace's Denali pulled up and screeched to a halt. He jumped out and ran up to the turned over Lincoln. He got down on his knees and looked inside. Everybody
looked dead.

By then everybody had exited the Denali and just stood around watching. As Ace grabbed Amaya's limp wrist through the window and tried to check for a pulse, it was shallow, but there was definitely one there. Ace turned around.

"Fuck ya'll dumb ass nigga fuckin' standin' around for? Call a fuckin' ambulance!'!" ..

To Be Continued…..

ABOUT THE AUTHOR

Young Hope Also Known As Benny Franco is a 25 year old entrepreneur who founded the company "Real Niggas N-Corporated" in 2012. RNC is a muli-tasked company that includes music production, clothing and graphic design as well as book publishing. Playin' For Keeps is the second publication from Young Hope.

www.ingramcontent.com/pod-product-compliance
Lightning Source LLC
Chambersburg PA
CBHW071307110426
42743CB00042B/1204